PRAISE FOR *BABEL*

'*Blockchain Babel* is a sobering, intelligent and audacious take on clarifying blockchain's many myths and misunderstandings. Every banking executive should read this book.'
John Waupsh, author of *Bankruption* and Chief Innovation Officer, Kasasa

'This book helps to disentangle the hype and get a clean glance on to a technology whose real business potential we have merely scratched so far.'
Georg Hauer, General Manager Austria, N26 Group

'*Blockchain Babel* is how all books on blockchain should be: well-balanced, myth-debunking, thought-provoking and entertaining enough to get you through to the end! A must-read guide for those who want to know more about blockchain technology – beyond the hype – and the way it will disrupt (or not!) the financial services sector globally.'
Markos Zachariadis, Associate Professor of Information Systems and Management, Warwick Business School, University of Warwick, and Fintech Research Fellow at the Cambridge Centre for Digital Innovation, University of Cambridge

'*Blockchain Babel* breaks the most common myths concerning blockchain technology in a smart and comprehensible manner. In this wonderful book, Pejic shapes a new understanding of the future development of blockchain technology.'
Philipp Sandner, Head of the Frankfurt School Blockchain Center, Frankfurt School of Finance and Management

'Igor Pejic takes an inside look at the crypto craze gold rush that is challenging banks, and peers around the corner at the complex world of international finance. Buckle up for a remarkable and intriguing blockchain ride that will forever change the payment system and slice across all industries. A powerful read and examination of the blockchain revolution unfolding before us now.'
Stephen G Andrews, Community Bank President and Fintech enthusiast

'The number of publications on blockchain technology coming out every day can be measured in metres of bookshelves right now. All the more remarkable is Igor Peijc's book, as it is highly informative, full of substance and engaging to read, despite the subject's complexity. Whether you want to get a good overview or dig in deep into the matter, you can get both out of this book. After reading this, blockchain will no longer be a mystery to you.'
Barbara Stöttinger, Dean, WU Executive Academy, Vienna

'In his riveting, yet analytic account of blockchain, Igor Pejic is shaping a new understanding of the technology that will transform banking and business. *Blockchain Babel* is a powerful compass to navigate the vast seas of crypto-literature.'
Jürgen Kob, Board Member of various companies and FinFluencer

'Igor Pejic has written one of the most comprehensive books about blockchain, in a clear and precise manner. It's a must-read for anyone involved in future business developments if they don't want to miss the blockchain revolution.'
Marc Toledo, Managing Director, Bit4you.io

Blockchain Babel

The crypto craze and the challenge to business

Igor Pejic

Kogan Page
INSPIRE

First published in Great Britain and the United States in 2019 by Kogan Page Limited

2nd Floor, 45 Gee Street
London
EC1V 3RS
United Kingdom

122 W 27th St, 10th Floor
New York, NY 10001
USA

4737/23 Ansari Road
Daryaganj
New Delhi 110002
India

www.koganpage.com

ISBNs

Hardback 978 0 7494 9798 9
Paperback 978 0 7494 8416 3
Ebook 978 0 7494 8417 0

British Library Cataloguing-in-Publication Data

A CIP record for this book is available from the British Library.

Library of Congress Cataloging-in-Publication Data

A CIP record for this book is available from the Library of Congress.

Typeset by Integra Software Services, Pondicherry
Print production managed by Jellyfish
Printed and bound by CPI Group (UK) Ltd, Croydon CR0 4YY

To my family and my wife

Contents

About the author

Igor Pejic has held different management positions in banking and payments, most recently as the Head of Marketing at BNP Paribas PF AT, part of Europe's largest banking group. He has advised Fortune 100 companies and taught at the University of Vienna, from which he also holds three degrees: an MA in English Linguistics, as well as a BA and MA in Journalism. Additionally, he completed an MBA at the WU Executive Academy.

As an ex-business journalist, he regularly comments on payments, banking, and tech-driven shifts in the media. McKinsey and the *Financial Times* voted him as one of three finalists in the Bracken Bower Prize in 2016 for his work on blockchain, which has resulted in this book.

Introduction

Welcome to the cryptocurrency craze

'Silicon Valley is coming', JP Morgan Chase CEO Jamie Dimon (2015) admonished the bank's shareholders. Though avoiding its name, he was referring to the blockchain, the technology behind bitcoin. This technology has the potential to force the finance industry through a change unseen for centuries.

The blockchain is a computer protocol enabling distributed ledgers and promising almost instantaneous and near free-value transactions. Money and assets can be moved without a central authority; validation is performed via a peer-to-peer network without the need for powerful intermediaries to authenticate or settle transactions.

The ground-breaking technology is no longer a fad favoured by nefarious wheelers and dealers. While bitcoin is still the first and best-known blockchain, the hunt for the killer application is in full swing. Following an explosion of fintech start-ups in the last five years, thousands of them are now hounding the industry that fuels the global economy. Investors keep injecting capital at an unprecedented speed, but at fintech and payments conferences, the blue jeans of Silicon Valley have given way to the suits of Wall Street. Start-ups are managed by experienced executives of big banks, while an impressive list of companies is lining up behind initiatives such as the R3 CEV consortium, a collaboration of leading financial institutions to define a common blockchain standard between them. The Hyperledger Project has a similar goal for business applications. As early as 2015, a study by Greenwich Associates found that 94 per cent of Wall Street bankers believed the blockchain had the potential to change the finance sector forever (Leising, 2015). We are seeing an industry collectively rising to combat the threat of a Kodak moment on their turf, with bankers and their ilk rushing to become the main purveyors of a future cashless world.

The hunt for the killer application is in full swing.

Banks are not the only ones whose imagination has been sparked. IT giants, journalists, entrepreneurs and venture capitalists alike are in a gold-rush mood. Academic research on bitcoin is skyrocketing. Publications in major research journals rose 267 per cent in two years, according to CoinDesk, a cryptocurrency news portal (Hileman, 2016). Magazines and institutes dedicated to the new technology mushroom across the globe, including at leading global institutions such as the 'Digital Currency Initiative' at the MIT Media Lab. The reason for this hype is clear: we are talking about a technology that, according to Spanish bank Santander, could save banks US $15–20 billion a year from 2022 onwards – even without altering the business model (Santander InnoVentures, Oliver Wyman and Anthemis, 2015). It is difficult to quantify what its effects might be if its potential is fully unlocked. While many see an unprecedented potential in the blockchain, existing companies behind payment processors, wire transfer services and credit card companies fret for their core business. They are right to be worried. The insurgents that are coming are not just another PayPal. As PayPal grew in record time it swallowed a large part of the profits pie, but it did this simply by adding another layer on top of the existing financial system. The blockchain, on the other hand, will be able to change the system from the ground up. Yes, banks and other incumbents are aware that the gauntlet has been thrown to them, yet the outcome is far from clear. After all, history has shown how easily companies can be paralysed by not keeping up with the times. Inertia blocks them, legacy systems drown them. But can start-ups really continue their impressive winning streak and dethrone the tight cartel of money giants? What role will cloud giants and data behemoths play? Google, Apple and Amazon are the only companies on a level with the financial giants.

Banks and other incumbents are aware that the gauntlet has been thrown to them.

Blockchain commentators – a mixed lot of tech-evangelists, anarcho-libertarians and industry experts – tend to have very strong and differing opinions about the future of the technology. However, while everybody in IT and banking seems to have an opinion on the blockchain, there is little systematic research, or strategic analysis. This book sets out to fill this void. Research about blockchain technology, financial history, innovation theory, competitive dynamics and management strategy is interwoven to produce a view that shows the big picture. Even the best historian cannot predict the future, and no management guru will give you advice for which they will accept liability. Both will couch their analyses in officialese and management jargon, but you can use the robust parts of their counsel to make an informed decision. Innovation patterns repeat themselves. Market mechanisms are reliable over time and geographies. As game-changing as the blockchain could be, it is not the first novelty to hit the world. *Blockchain Babel* aims to break down the barrier between pioneer enthusiasm and academic soberness to give actionable, but substantiated, strategic guidance.

The book debunks seven common myths that underpin almost each discussion about the blockchain. These myths not only persist, but they have hijacked media and pundits alike. They follow a consistent internal logic, selectively point out parallels to well-known examples, fit the zeitgeist and tap into a global anti-banking sentiment. But empirical evidence can silence the din. Pointing out the logical flaws and discrepancies is crucial for decision makers to get a more realistic picture of the opportunities and challenges ahead. The attempt seems worth making if it can bring the technology into sharper focus in the mind's eye of the general reader, and yes, even blockchain experts.

The myths also serve to structure the book – each chapter refutes one misconception. I start with clarifying the societal impact and the technological principles, move on to the hunt for the new competitive advantage and innovative business models, before finally addressing the question of whether the blockchain really has the potential to boost the economy and slash inequality.

The transformational power of blockchain technology is by no means limited to the finance sector. It reaches from secure identification and e-voting, to new compensation models for artists and media professionals, all the way to smart contracts and property rights. Governments are already involved in the new technology: the British-launched D5 group of nations searches for digital alternatives to fiat currencies, while the Pentagon works on a blockchain-based messaging system. Experts agree: we are witnessing the birth of the internet all over again. Yet this book confines its scope to the very heart of the blockchain protocol: the banking industry. The financial system is the lifeblood of our economy, and what happens there is felt in every other industry. As an example, micropayments and smart contracts (smart contracts are when contracts are encoded onto a blockchain and enforced automatically by the algorithm) depend on the payment blockchain protocol. Above all, if capital becomes cheaper and access to it easier, this can unleash immense economic growth and provide huge potential for global innovation.

In computer code we trust

Ask average business-press readers what they know about blockchain, and they will tell you it has something to do with bitcoins and payments. Their knowledge will culminate in either the conclusion that it is a bubble or that it will revolutionize finance. Blockchain enthusiasts will correct this claim: 'The technology will change *every* industry from the ground up.' Gesturing enthusiastically, they will add that a crypto coin can be built for everything. Yet, pressed for details on how it works, most will either give a very superficial answer or will drown in technical details. It's true that it is very difficult to pack the details of the technology into an executive summary. Hence, crafty commentators resort to analogies. Blockchain has been called the 'Internet of Money' (Swan, 2015) and the 'e-mail for money' (Blythe Masters quoted in Wild, Arnold and Stafford, 2015). It has been compared to operating systems such as Windows or Android (*The Economist*, 2016), and likened to the internet itself, the difference being that instead of connecting information it connects value (Tapscott and Tapscott, 2016). These comparisons provide an important starting point in understanding blockchain; they all regard it as an underlying structure, a new network on which applications for monetary transactions can run.

OK, so blockchain is a platform with applications. But what makes it so different to current payment and transaction systems? The key phrase here that is repeated like a never-ending mantra is *distributed ledger technology*.[1] Sets of records are not kept and updated by a central authority or privileged intermediaries such as credit-card companies or processors, but distributed across different computer nodes over the globe. It is a network based on peer-to-peer (P2P) technology. This leads to a host of features that distinguish the blockchain system from current banking networks. First, it does away with any kind of intermediaries. Let's use another analogy to explain this. You can think of a blockchain application in terms of an online, collaborative Microsoft Excel document that everyone in the network can fill with additional lines denominating a transaction. There is no administrator validating the changes and storing a master copy in their systems. Instead, the file is stored on every computer in the network. As soon as your new line is confirmed by the other participants, it is saved and the copy on each computer is updated. However – and this is another distinctive feature of the blockchain – nothing can be deleted or modified. At least, not unless a nightmare scenario happens in which more than 50 per cent of the nodes conspire to change the ledger's history. Later we will see that, although this scenario is unlikely, it is more probable than any bitcoin enthusiast is ready to admit. This irreversibility has earned the blockchain the reputation of an 'an unimpeachable record keeper' (Umeh, 2016).

Having no central authority also means no one is checking on the nodes' real identities. Though participants can see the transaction history on the ledger, only metadata and pseudonyms of the transacting parties are visible. Since its inception bitcoin has been linked to crime and the dark web; tax evasion and drug trafficking are the least troublesome allegations levelled against it. This negative image is also rubbing off on the technology behind bitcoin, which is seen as guilty by association. This is another common misbelief as the blockchain can indeed be used in a controlled environment. Compare it to Napster, the first P2P music-sharing platform. Though it operated outside the legally allowed boundaries and was shut down, it gave rise to a host of other P2P file-sharing platforms, including legitimate ones such as Spotify (*The Economist*, 2015).

Bitcoin and the beginnings of the blockchain

Blockchain technology was described for the first time in the infamous paper by Satoshi Nakamoto in 2008. The paper is infamous because never before had bitcoin, blockchain or the mechanisms behind them been described or heard of. Yet, to this day no one knows the real identity of the author(s) who explained to the world the workings of bitcoin, the first cryptocurrency. No one knows what the anonymous inventor(s)' motives were, how many bitcoins they still own, and what kind of influence they might still have over the blockchain community a decade on. Tenacious rumours persist that Nakamoto is a Russian or Chinese agent, a famous cryptographer, one of the current crypto power-brokers, or even a celebrity (such as Elon Musk).

Blockchain was initially only developed as an enabler for bitcoin and still is often used to denominate the same. It is important to differentiate between bitcoin, its blockchain, and the blockchain idea in general. Bitcoin is a virtual currency. It has a specific blockchain, while other cryptocurrencies such as Ethereum have their own blockchains. Each of these blockchains act as the ledger that keeps track of the virtual coins' transactions. So while bitcoin is impossible without the blockchain, blockchain *is* possible without bitcoin.

It is important to differentiate between bitcoin, its blockchain, and the blockchain idea in general.

Using bitcoin to illustrate how the blockchain works

If this is all sounding a bit too complex, you are not alone. The abstractness and complexity of the bitcoin and blockchain mechanisms can be offputting and will need to be minimized if the applications are to go mainstream. For users to entrust their hard-earned money to the bitcoin system, they will need first to understand how its basic principles make it as secure as the current system. This is where it gets tricky, so let's take a more detailed look at the bitcoin system to illustrate how the blockchain works.

To get started, every participant in the network must download the bitcoin protocol onto their computer. A copy of the bitcoin blockchain is then saved to the hard drive. By loading the program onto the new network-member's device it is turned into a new node. Similar to the volunteer network BitTorrent, the node becomes part of a shared database. This distributed nature of the database makes it difficult for states or other regulatory bodies to get hold of such networks.

To hold and use bitcoins and other virtual currencies, users also need wallets. Misleading as it may sound, a wallet is not a physical object that holds your possessions, but is software that allows you to access your value on the blockchain. *Key* is a more appropriate term. Imagine a browser that enables you to enter the web. Wallets work on the same principle. The only difference is that in blockchain-based transactions the system does not identify the user via an IP address, but a pseudonymous code that no human can remember. When you transfer money to someone, your wallet sends a request to trigger a decrease of the value in your wallet and simultaneously a value increase in the other party's wallet. The nodes – or miners as they are called in bitcoin speak – then check their respective copy of the ledger to see if the initiator of the transaction owns the necessary monetary amount. They bundle the transaction together with other reputable remittances to create a new block that is to be attached to the chain of blocks generated by past transactions. This is how the blockchain gets its name.

Now for the really clever bit, the wow factor in terms of pseudonymity and security. This is also where it gets more technically complex, so bear with me. Via another program each transaction is encrypted into a so-called 'hash' value that is unique and has a uniform length. Hashing simply means that the original information is transformed into a code via mathematical scrambling. This is done with one-way cryptography; so if someone only has the hash, they cannot find the initial input variables. As mentioned, each hash is unique, and it can be allocated to a specific transaction. Multiple hash values generated from multiple transactions are then bundled into a system called the Merkle Tree. After being

FIGURE 0.1 Simplified illustration of the block set-up and hashing mechanism

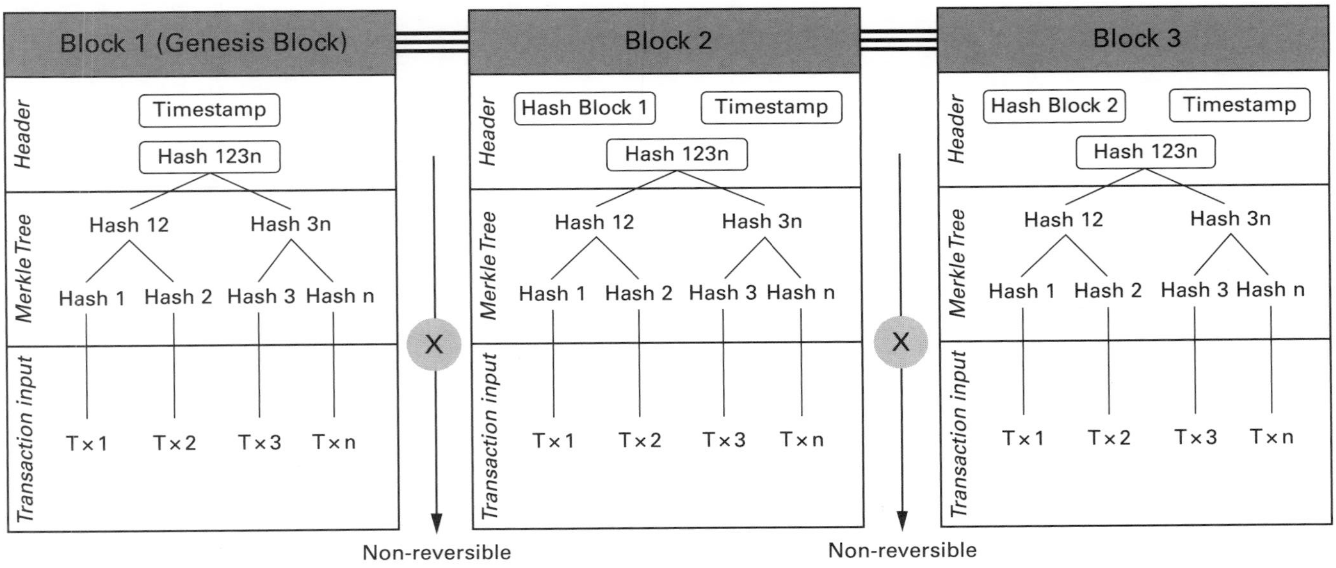

Block 1 (Genesis Block)
Header
Timestamp
Hash 123n
Merkle Tree
Hash 12
Hash 3n
Hash 1 Hash 2 Hash 3 Hash n
Transaction input
T×1 T×2 T×3 T×n

Non-reversible

Block 2
Header
Hash Block 1
Timestamp
Hash 123n
Merkle Tree
Hash 12
Hash 3n
Hash 1 Hash 2 Hash 3 Hash n
Transaction input
T×1 T×2 T×3 T×n

Non-reversible

Block 3
Header
Hash Block 2
Timestamp
Hash 123n
Merkle Tree
Hash 12
Hash 3n
Hash 1 Hash 2 Hash 3 Hash n
Transaction input
T×1 T×2 T×3 T×n

bundled together, a block's header is created. The header is a value that also includes the hash of the previous block on the chain, and this is where the chain becomes tamper-proof. Because the header of a block refers to the previous one, altering the preceding block becomes impossible without altering all subsequent blocks (Franco, 2015). Each block is also stamped with the exact date and time, which means that no single bitcoin can be used twice (Nakamoto, 2008). Figure 0.1 shows how the blocks and the hash values are built.

The transaction is not yet completed, however. A mathematical puzzle is built around the newly generated block header, once again using the hash function. For the transactions to be verified and the block added to the chain, nodes must solve the puzzle. Here the nodes' main service is not transaction validation; every node of the network can do that. What miners do when solving puzzles and dedicating computing power is to decide which transaction to include in each block; they have 'the power to vote on the truth' (Tapscott and Tapscott, 2016).

So how is this puzzle solved? This depends on the specific blockchain. In the bitcoin system, nodes do so by using brute force, ie they try to arrive at the right result via trial and error, plugging in one solution after the other. The possibilities for the right solutions are in the trillions. Ergo, the higher the computing power, the higher the likelihood of solving the block first because nodes can plug in trial values faster – and the reward is high. The node that first hits the right solution pockets freshly minted bitcoins. Before the winning node gets the credit, however, the other miners have to verify the proposed solution. Verification can be performed quickly once you have the correct value. The nodes just plug the value into the equation and can check it instantly. The ledger is then updated accordingly with all the transactions inside the new block. The hash that was generated on the basis of the header is saved as part of the ledger and is referenced by the next block that wants to link to the chain (Franco, 2015). In Figure 0.2 you can see a stripped-down

FIGURE 0.2 The process of adding new blocks to the chain

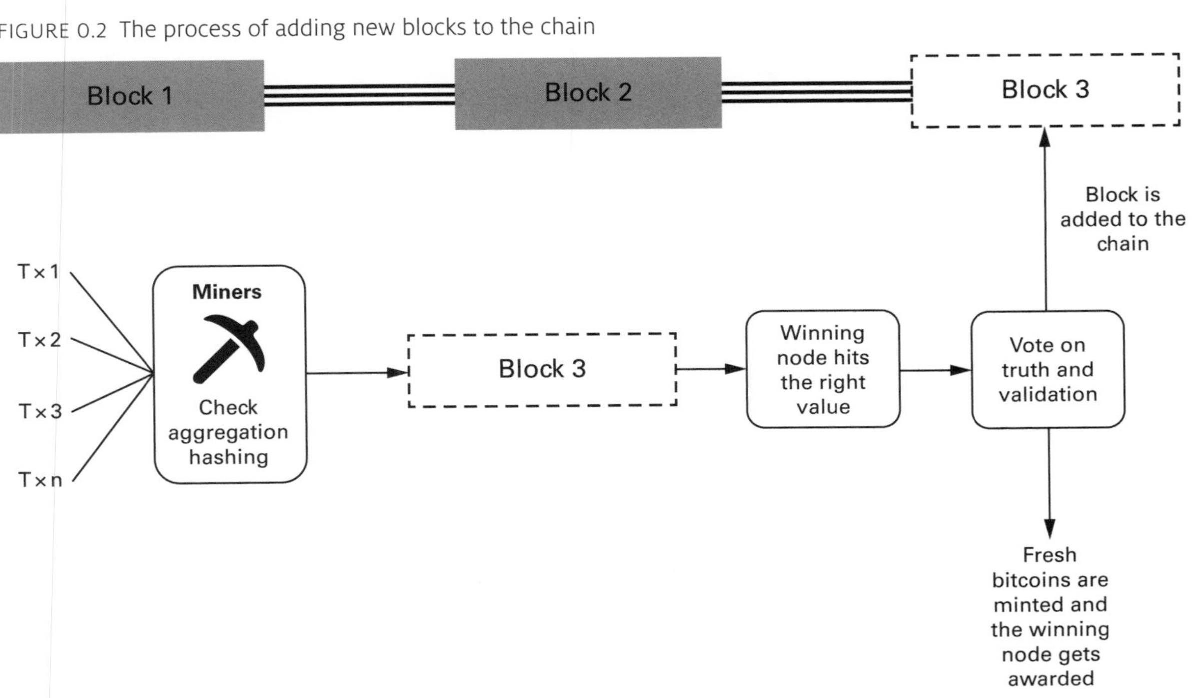

version of the process of block generation and validation. It is important to remember at this point that the blockchain is not a store of accounts, but a list recording all transactions in its history.

This section has been dubbed 'In computer code we trust', alluding to the creed enshrined on US dollar bills. However, with cryptocurrencies trust is not put in God, a central bank, or any bank for that matter. The idea of one privileged authority deciding on the truth yields to decentralized consensus – this was Nakamoto's ground-breaking innovation in 2008 and a complete conceptual shift. Yet if blockchain is going to go mainstream, the absence of authority is arguably an unsustainable concept, both commercially and technically. Commercially, you need authorities – banks, for instance – to impose the technology onto the mass market or it will stay a niche forever. Technically, no absolutely distributed system can efficiently master the crucial challenge that every payment system faces: ensuring money is not spent twice.

How it works – overcoming the double-spent problem

We keep money and documents not because the paper is worth so much, but because we trust that others will also recognize its worth. Today, most monetary value has no representation in bills or coins. But the digitalization of money and assets faces a tremendous problem that other domains do not: unlike a photograph or PDF, or even a university diploma or birth certificate, the value of money would vanish instantly if it could be copied during a transaction. In other words, how can we make sure that once money is received by another party, it also disappears in the account of the sending party and is not just multiplied?

The value of money would vanish instantly if it could be copied during a transaction.

The way this problem is solved in the current banking system is that every transaction is channelled through a third party. A money transfer service, a bank, a governmental body, a credit-card company. Their task is to run each transaction through a centralized database and update it accordingly, making the transaction cycle a resource-intensive process that takes days, sometimes weeks.

In the past half century technological development has triggered two noteworthy changes to payments and financial transactions. First, ledgers have been moved from paper to electronic. This boosted the speed of transactions and sent down operational risk. Second, innovation such as mobile payment was enabled by the mass proliferation of smartphones and put a personal bank-counter into everyone's pocket. Yet the underlying transaction logic remains, and a multilayered structure of intermediaries verifies each step. Every bank has master ledgers where an individual's possession is stored (Ali *et al*, 2014). The master file of an account contains not only a customer's account balance but their transaction history of the last 60 days, 90 days, or whatever other period the bank deems suitable. Also, there are a number of ledgers for tracking cash and assets through the system, as well as journals that hold transactions that were received from other sources but are not yet recorded in the ledger. Then there is an audit trail used to document each step of each actor along the way. On top sits processing software that connects all those ledgers, master files and journals. Audit processes ensure a frictionless operation between them (Peters and Panayi, 2015). Banks also hold accounts that are recorded in a central body's ledger, for example a central bank. Underpinning the entire transactions system is the SWIFT (Society for Worldwide Interbank Financial Telecommunication) network with its financial platform SwiftNet, a private exchange network not built on P2P trust like the blockchain, but on a centralized model. All these processes and actors obviously come at a cost. The fee for remittances is 8–9 per cent of the transaction value, whereas the transaction fee for bitcoin is 0.01–0.05 per cent (Peters and Panayi, 2015). At least that was what the world's bitcoin enthusiasts imagined. Within three years, as bitcoin was pushed towards its scalability limits, fees soared to around US $19 per transaction (Hertig, 2018). Scalability, however, is only a show-stopper for bitcoin, not for the blockchain. The point is that the blockchain mechanism is slimmed down and with the right technical set-up it can trim costs to the bone.

The cost of transactions is not just monetary, however. Time is also a major factor. Every transaction comprises three steps. It starts with the authorization at the time of purchase or wire transfer. This can be the terminal at a grocery store verifying your chip card and its available amount, or a four-digit code sent by text message to validate a bank wire. Authorization runs through at least the issuing bank, the acquiring bank and most probably a processor and credit-card network. Yet it happens within seconds. The second stage is the clearing, which is when two parties update their accounts and provision for transferring money or securities. This stage takes one day to be completed. When the money and the securities are actually exchanged we talk about settlement, the third and ultimate stage of the transaction cycle. Settlement is the most problematic phase. An in-store credit-card payment passes through multiple intermediaries and is authorized within seconds, but it can be days until settlement occurs. Remittance settlement is even worse. Depending on where the acquiring account is located it may take up to a week.

On the blockchain there is just one system. One ledger. There is no delay in settlement; it takes no longer than authorization and clearing. And the double-spent problem? Each bitcoin is subject to a mechanism called digital time stamping. Once time-stamped during a transaction, a bitcoin can never be used again. But is it really that easy? And if it is, why don't incumbents just time-stamp their digital value tokens? The truth is, the consensus among the network nodes comes with a price tag. There are different algorithmic paths to agreement. Bitcoin works with the proof-of-work mechanism. To create the next block in the chain and thus receive a reward, miners have to find the unique fingerprint of a file, the aforementioned hash. They have to be the first to solve a mathematical puzzle. In the proof-of-work mechanism those puzzles can only be solved by trial-and-error approaches. This brute force approach is the best known, but it comes with two major disadvantages.

First, the proof-of-work-principle kills operational scalability. The number of transactions it can perform in a given time is low and limited. This is why bitcoin is not the blockchain's killer application and why it will never seriously threaten to displace incumbents. Nakamoto limited the block size to one megabyte, which corresponds to around 1,400 transactions per block or around seven transactions per second. As a comparison, Visa handles 1,736 transactions per second only in the United States. The average daily transaction volume for bitcoin is US $289 million as compared to $17.559 million of Visa, $9,863 million of MasterCard, or $7.562 million through China Union Pay (Coinometrics, 2015). Programmers are coming up with solutions such as the Bitcoin Lightening Network, but these are forlorn efforts as bitcoin was never set up to go mainstream. Before we look at the promising alternatives to proof-of-work, there is another reason why bitcoin must not be the flagbearer of blockchain enthusiasts. As the name of the mechanism hints at, nodes compete against each other by putting immense computing power to work, racing towards the right solution. Hashing burns a lot of electricity. How much is a lot? Go ahead, take a guess – and don't forget, bitcoin handles seven transactions per second instead of the thousands currently managed by the credit-card networks. Is its energy consumption comparable to a medium-sized company? An international mega-company? A city even? Unfortunately, none of those. The answer is much grimmer. Currently, the bitcoin network gobbles as much energy as the entire Irish economy (Walport, 2016), though these estimates vary and others have compared it to the consumption of Cyprus (Kaminska, 2014). This is just the electricity bill. On top of this, most mining equipment has to be trashed after three to six months for the node to stay competitive, which is a tremendous burden for the environment (McCook, 2014). Sustainability was not high on Nakamoto's agenda.

Other blockchain applications and platforms, however, perform verification differently and make up for these shortcomings. Frontier, an app that runs on bitcoin's major competitor, the Ethereum blockchain, has opted for the proof-of-stake concept, meaning that nodes that have more interest in the success of the particular blockchain have more influence. If you own a large amount of the currency, you get more voting rights on the truth. So the weight of a node is not influenced by its computing power but is biased by other tokens. The major advantage is the energy efficiency. Nowadays verification mechanisms come in all sorts: the blockchain Stellar also uses the proof-of-stake mechanism, but relies on social networks. Then there are proof-of-capacity and proof-of-storage verification processes, whereby miners allocate hard-drive volume to finding the hash. Those systems use the dedicated resources to operate, which makes sense as the entire blockchain since its inception has to be saved and preserved. Blockchain enthusiasts also dream about connecting the billions of transactions that will be executed via smart contracts to the network. Their hope is that in an M2M-connected world where each home appliance has some kind of computing and storage power and is connected to an information grid, it will be possible to feed unutilized resources to the blockchain (Tapscott and Tapscott, 2016).

Security costs – and if we are going to pay for security, it should be to safeguard our money's value. But is the blockchain really that secure?

Unlocking the chain – too good to be secure?

One of blockchain's major selling points is that transactions are tamper proof, and its ledger is unhackable. The record can only be updated if the majority of nodes' computing power agrees. Fraud cannot happen, and, as each node sees all transactions, if it did happen everyone else in the network would see it. The system is based on the idea that individuals, whether they are part of the network or not, cannot be trusted, but they still manage to achieve consensus because of the incentive mechanism. People's actions are predictable because they are fuelled by self-interest. If a node goes rogue, it doesn't make a difference because the majority will have a ballot on the truth. The verification mechanism is secure and thus bitcoin is secure. Or so it was thought until 2014 when the Mt. Gox scandal shook the bitcoin world. Mt. Gox was a Tokyo-based bitcoin exchange launched four years earlier. At the time of the attack it had quickly soared to the world's largest trading exchange with 70 per cent of all bitcoin transactions being processed by it. In an unseen heist, US $450 million or 850,000 customer bitcoins were stolen in 2014, most of which never appeared again. Manipulated bots sent the bitcoin price on a rollercoaster ride. A lot of people lost a lot of money and the Bitcoin Foundation, the organization running the exchange, went bankrupt (Skinner, 2016). The US $450 million hack was no isolated incident: for example, when the Slovenian exchange Bitstamp was hacked, US $5 million was stolen (Umeh, 2016). Security holes like these led IT security expert Kaspersky Labs to conclude that it is possible to infest blockchain transactions with malware (Heires, 2016), which leads us to the question: is the blockchain that secure after all?

Bitcoin devotees believe that it was not the technology that let people down and cost bitcoin investors so dearly, but human mistakes. They do have a point. At the heart of blockchain technology is the mechanism ensuring that money is not spent twice,

Bitcoin devotees believe that it was not the technology that let people down and cost bitcoin investors so dearly, but human mistakes.

but security needs to be ensured on a much broader level. When we talk about security on the blockchain, in essence we talk about data integrity. This must include the entire life cycle of the data and must look at whether it is accurate, consistent and valid during *all* stages. I have pinpointed three risks that need to be considered: the availability of the ledger, data security offline (ie before/after the transaction), and data security online (ie during the transaction). For cryptocurrencies such as bitcoin there is a fourth peril: currency risk. Cryptocurrencies are radically different from fiat currency as they are not subject to inflation. One of Nakamoto's concerns was that by increasing the supply of bitcoins its value would decrease, which is why he capped the supply of total bitcoins at 21 million. The bitcoin currency has no central bank or Federal Reserve (FED) that can influence the amount of currency in circulation. Instead, the minting of new coins works according to a pre-determined mechanism. Per block that was completed and linked to the previous block, miners received 50 bitcoins in the first four years. The amount was halved after four subsequent years, and this halving mechanism will continue at the same pace until approximately 2140, the year the total number of bitcoins in circulation will be reached (Donnelly, 2016). Similar to shares in a start-up, this ensured early supporters had a large incentive to keep the network running. At the same time, though, this will lead to problems that traditional currencies don't have, for instance how to motivate miners to perform the authentication after 2140. Also, virtual currencies that are not anchored in real economies and have no national bank are subject to massive currency fluctuations – eg climbing 56 per cent in H1 2016 according to the CoinDesk USD Bitcoin Price Index (Bovaird, 2016).

Concentration of bitcoin ownership is another problem; 937 people own around half of all bitcoins in circulation (Wile, 2013). A detailed look at currency volatility is beyond the scope of this book, but readers who would like to find out more about topics such as inflation or the absence of a national bank will find a detailed discussion in *The Age of Cryptocurrency: How bitcoin and the blockchain are challenging the global economic order*, by Paul Vigna and Michael J Casey.

Let us now return to the three security dimensions that apply to all blockchains, whether they are underpinning digital or fiat currencies. The first dimension to look at is the availability of the system and the data. Here blockchain-based applications have an advantage to centralized systems. Distributed ledgers are more resilient. If a bank has an IT problem and cannot access its master ledger, it will not be able to perform money transfers or retrieve money before the problem is fixed. This would not be the case, however, if your money was stored on the blockchain. The replication of the database on any node ensures that, even if some nodes become unavailable, users have access. The security level will only drop in proportion to the loss of computing power.

How about the security when data is offline, in other words, not part of a current transaction? Blockchain defenders argue that in Mt. Gox and other scandals the problem was the storage and handling of the data. This is where the elimination of financial institutions from the network is felt; it puts increased responsibility on the individual. Electronic deposits held with commercial banks are more secure with regards to recoverability. If I lose my PIN code, it takes a few clicks to receive a new one. Once the private key of a blockchain account is lost, so are the digital assets and, even if the blockchain rids itself of financial intermediaries, there are other intermediaries that are inevitable for certain blockchain applications. The company CoinSpark, for example, acts as a blockchain notary. Yes, you do still need a notary, and an exchange. Your data – and thus possession – will still pass through a lot of hands and you need to trust they will store your data properly. At the end of the day, if for any reason your chattels are not paid out, you are not protected as a saver by any banking regulation. It is a risky bet.

So, during the transactions? Just like smart-card transactions, the blockchain technology relies on high-level encryption, namely on public key infrastructure (PKI). This is elaborate asymmetric cryptography in which the communicating parties use a private as well as a public key to ensure no one else can snoop on their communications. These keys are alphanumeric sequences. The public keys, as the name suggests, are known to everyone, the private ones only to the key holder. The recipient can only decipher the message if they have both. PKI slashes the risk of digital communication as it ensures the data sent is genuine and private. No one can interfere. No one can eavesdrop.

So communication is authentic and secure, but what if the mechanism gets tricked? What if the message sent is wrong to begin with because the nodes decide to vote a truth into reality that fits their ulterior goals? In bitcoin literature this scenario is known as the Sybil or identity-forging attack. As more than half of the computing power of the network is needed in order to do so, some also call it the 51 per cent attack. In theory, if anyone gets more than half of the nodes or computing power under control, they could rewrite the entire chain. It is not that easy though. Nakamoto built in three principles that guarantee bitcoin's security during the puzzle stage in which the nodes are looking for the right solution. The first is chance. Nodes use brute force to hit the right hash, trying one value after another. Hence, it cannot be predicted which miner will solve the puzzle and get to update the chain. The second safeguard is history. Each block is connected to the preceding one linking all the way to the genesis block (*The Economist*, 2015). Changing previous blocks would incur energy costs so high that any potential financial gain would be cancelled out. The longer the chain gets, the safer it is, and the computing power needed to alter it also increases (Tapscott and Tapscott, 2016). Changing a preceding transaction would change the hash, which is incorporated in all the subsequent blocks. So to modify one block in the past, you would also have to modify all blocks afterwards by redoing the proof-of-work for each of them (Nakamoto, 2008). Finally, the incentives scheme of bitcoin also favours an 'honest' vote on the truth. To receive the reward, nodes always work on the longest version, making it impossible to change the history on the ledger (*The Economist*, 2015). In reality, it is very unlikely that more than half of the computing power will join a conspiracy, especially since there are currently around 10,000 bitcoin nodes.[2]

There are other, more sceptical voices, many of which are particularly focused on blockchains that work with the proof-of-work mechanism. Mining bitcoins is not an equal playing field, and the inherent inequalities can result in monopolistic tensions. Selfish miners can join together to increase their likelihood of being rewarded. Thus, other miners will join the largest conglomerate out of self-interest and possibly form a node larger than 50 per cent; this almost happened in the past (Eyal and Gün Sirer, 2014). Remember: it is not about getting the majority of nodes, but of computing power. Mega-sized mining factories have much higher voting share than the home PC you converted into a node.

In the end, the real question is not whether blockchain technology is completely secure, but whether it is more secure than the current system. In the old days, when bank robberies involved guns and getaway cars there was no illusion of absolute security – not even for the cash stashed away behind the doors of heavy-steel vaults. Today, images of hackers hammering some illegible code into their keyboards do not tend to make the headlines, but banking coups do persist, and thieves can grab far more money now than any masked bandit with a revolver could have done in times gone by. In 2016 banking-card fraud alone bled over US $22.80 billion annually from the banking industry. That is 7.15 cents per every $100 of total volume – and the trend is negative. The share is up from 6.97 cents per $100 in 2015 or from 4.46 cents in 2010 (The Nilson Report, 2017). Even the SWIFT network, which enables monetary transactions between 11,000 financial institutions worldwide, has been subject to hacking in the past. In one heist, banks in Bangladesh and Ecuador lost US $90 million (Burne and Sidel, 2017). One weak spot is the existing data management infrastructure built on IT-legacy systems. Instead of replacing outdated software, new systems are simply added on to it, increasing cost, complexity and vulnerability. The more IT systems and interfaces you have under your control, the more possibilities and vulnerabilities you have to entice would-be attackers. No fortress is unconquerable in the digital world. Consider this: on average there are 10–15 mistakes per 1,000 lines of code. Leading software companies can push it down to 0.5 mistakes, but there will always be bugs that hackers can exploit (*The Economist*, 2017). So each IT legacy that is trashed slashes the number of lines of code. The blockchain helps to do exactly that. You are now equipped with the knowledge to convince your chief security officer. So far, so good. But here comes the real challenge: are the customers ready?

Banking coups do persist.

Notes

1 Often, blockchains are equated with distributed ledgers, but this is not entirely correct. The actual distributed ledgers are the protocols sitting on top of the blockchain, thus the blockchain itself is not the ledger, but the mechanism for transaction validation (ie to reach the consensus between the different nodes in the ledger).

2 11,147 to be exact (15 February 2018) according to https://bitnodes.21.co/

CHAPTER ONE

Blockchain, Bitcoin and Distributed Ledgers – Disentangling the Hype

Myth: 'The blockchain is the second generation of the internet, equal in heft.'

Why stop with banking? The dream of blockchain 2.0

Those who have followed blockchain over recent years will have noticed that it has turned from an unknown, online technology enabling transactions into a panacea for all ills. Once you have a hammer in your hand everything suddenly looks like a nail. Blockchain is the hammer. Eight major categories of blockchain applications have been identified:

- general applications;
- cryptocurrencies;

- financial transactions;
- public records;
- identification;
- attestation;
- physical asset keys; and
- intangible assets. (Swan, 2015)

Each of the above is said to have the potential to revolutionize not only an industry, but often the entire economy. Take the safeguarding of property rights as an example. In many less developed countries property rights are often endangered due to an unchecked ruler, a corrupt judicial system and – here comes the code word for blockchain enthusiast – a malleable property ledger. If you oppose the predominant political system, if a member of the ruling class needs your land to give it to a person of their blood or ethnicity, or a king wants your property to build a highway, you don't stand a chance. The record is changed and your possession is no longer yours (Tapscott and Tapscott, 2016). This is bitter for the individual, but also for the economy as a whole. It makes it harder to use land or other real estate as collateral, for instance to build a new business, which in turn diminishes investment and impacts employment levels (*The Economist*, 2015). Also, foreigners will think twice before investing in that country.

Another annoyance the blockchain could remedy is the misuse of intellectual property rights. It will, its proponents tell us, make micropayments possible and feasible. Artists, journalists and movie creators can be paid by cents instead of having their content illegally downloaded. Blockchain could also revolutionize secure digital-identity verification. Voting is a widely described example. Putting identities on the blockchain will make it tamper proof and foster democracy. No longer will governing parties be able to manipulate voting cards or hackers meddle in elections. The immutable ledger also ensures that foreign aid reaches its target (Tapscott and Tapscott, 2016) or that electronic patient records in the health sector are secured

(Baxendale, 2016). Governments across the world have realized the potential and are trying to harness it. This is especially true of the D5 Group of Nations (Estonia, the UK, Israel, New Zealand, South Korea), which is striving to implement blockchain-related technologies. Estonia launched services such as e-tax or e-business registers based on distributed ledger technology verification (Walport, 2016).

Not only are these possibilities intriguing, but they are also simplistic. Could a piece of code really prevent an African dictator from usurping a farmer's land to build a highway? Would users really want to go through the hassle of making a transaction every time they read an article, just to give the author a fraction of a cent? As for voter-ID, how would you ensure the person entering the alphanumeric sequence is really the person whose face is on the ID? This technological determinism assumes that one tool will in itself make the world a better place. There is no doubt that the blockchain is powerful, but how markets act on it will be even more so.

There is no doubt that the blockchain is powerful, but how markets act on it will be even more so.

This is where 'smart contracts' come in. Everything discussed so far can be subsumed under the term blockchain 1.0. Smart contracts take the blockchain to the next level: blockchain 2.0 (Swan, 2015). An often quoted example is the car that locks its doors if the car's owner fails to pay the monthly lease. Contractual conditions are encoded into the algorithm and executed automatically instead of having a human judge and executor. The smart contract idea is nothing new, and was first discussed in the 1990s (Szabo, 1997), but it was only after the advent of the blockchain that a possible technological footing emerged. A good example of a blockchain platform that uses smart contracts is Ethereum. Ethereum is a platform built on a powerful blockchain. This platform runs apps that move around value and safeguard ownership. By using smart contracts technology, Ethereum has become one of the top blockchain projects; the company saw its share price skyrocket from US $11.29 on 5 January 2017 to $1,044.54 exactly one year later (Coinmarketcap, 2018). Meanwhile, sensors are making their way into almost every device. Cars and smartphones are bursting with them – and who would have thought five years ago that fridges would be made up of sensors that are connected to the internet and can automatically order food by monitoring stock and diet patterns? We are at the very beginning of the connected-device economy. The research firm Gartner (2015) estimates that the internet of things (IoT) in 2020 will count a staggering 20.8 billion connected devices, up from 'only' 6.4 billion in 2016. This exploding number gets harder to manage centrally every day. Even incumbents like IBM acknowledge that a centralized model will not work in the IoT world, claiming that it is 'time for the cloud to move from the data centre to your doorknob' (Pureswaran and Brody, 2015). To manage a global system of interconnected smart devices at reasonable costs, a trustless, P2P system is needed. As the blockchain offers decentralized consensus, the authors of the IBM report conclude that blockchain is not only the technology to facilitate the transactions, but also the coordination between the devices.

This explosion of applications has also been boosted by the invention of a new investment vehicle: Initial Coin Offerings (ICOs). ICOs can be used to raise capital for a new crypto coin or token by which early investors purchase coins and hope their value will balloon. It is comparable to a company's stocks, but you do not receive dividends. Some ICOs can even equip the holder with voting power in the network, because their technical basis privileges nodes with a stake in the particular token.

So with all these exciting new possibilities, why does *Blockchain Babel* focus on the banking sector? First, even smart contracts rely on the blockchain to serve as the new (micro) payment layer of the economy. Second, the finance industry often paves the way for other sectors in terms of new business models, market dynamics and capital. If the blockchain manages to free tied-up capital, it could trigger a global investment splurge. Third, there seems to be a consensus among blockchain experts that finance will be the central area to be transformed. In its annual survey CoinDesk (Hileman, 2016) interviewed thought leaders and found 77 per cent of them convinced that finance would be the domain most affected by the blockchain, whilst 54 per cent of them felt that identity would see the biggest impact, and a mere 38 per cent thought it would be property titles.

Finance as blockchain's weather vane

But even when we talk about blockchain and finance, the possibilities seem endless. Cryptocurrencies, transactions and remittances are just the most imminent application possibilities. Financial blockchains fall into one of four groups: retail payments, wholesale payments, capital markets and securities servicing (Wyman and Euroclear, 2016). Retail payments are the best known and most important. Most applications fall in this category, and they underpin the other groups. They comprise parallel currencies, including crypto and traditional currencies, as well as remittances and associated wallets. Wholesale payments include the overhauling of banking networks and cross-border financing. Thanks to the blockchain, money between companies can be moved easily even across states. Blockchain will also impact capital markets and securities servicing, primarily in the settlement of securities and asset documentation. Finally, blockchain can be used in trade finance and transaction banking, including supply chain and receivables finance, as well as commodities trade finance. We're not talking about scenarios in the distant future here; NASDAQ has already built a blockchain-based solution called NASDAQ Linq that helps companies to represent share ownership digitally (NASDAQ, 2016). So this list shows the wealth of application fields; blockchain is a panacea. Yet the reason I highlight this is not to underline its importance, but to shed light on a central problem that will emerge once loans, bonds, stocks and derivatives join the payments transformation on the blockchain: interoperability. By this I mean that different blockchains will be in use and they should all be compatible. Companies, and financial institutions in particular, will be part of multiple blockchain-based ledgers – a foreign exchange (FX) network, a bond network, a bitcoin network, and so on. This tells us two things. First, the only way to harness the entire potential of the new technology is for a consortium of IT companies and financial institutions to come together and define shared standards. One such effort is already under way, namely the Linux-led Hyperledger Project. Hardware, software platforms and applications need to be in line. Second, no application will be able to lead in isolation in the blockchain world; a decisive selling point for any application will be the ease with which it can be integrated into other systems.

For the blockchain, finance is, and probably always will be, the weather vane, and, as we have just seen, construction sites in financial services abound. So is there really any need to bother with other application fields such as e-voting? The main argument I want to make with this chapter is that those in the finance industry must not see the new technology as an attack or simply an opportunity to trim down the current IT systems. Such a limited view, one that sees the technology simply in terms of delivering cheaper financial services, would overlook a core potential competitive advantage. Banks, credit-card companies and the like are institutions of trust. For centuries people have entrusted them with their most valuable material possessions. With the

For the blockchain, finance is, and probably always will be, the weather vane.

blockchain they get a tool to use this trust and break into new markets. Many of those markets are highly profitable for small and specialized companies. Bear in mind that the financial dimension of the blockchain underpins many other fields, so a blockchain strategy must not end with monetary transactions. But before we dive into strategy, let's look at the mechanisms that breathe trust into all these diverse fields.

The second shot at electronic money and why this time it might actually work

Pioneers get the arrows, settlers get the land. That is a truth that so many headline-capturing trailblazers have experienced first-hand. Great visionaries and breakthrough inventors come in all shapes and sizes, but there is one thing they need above all else: the right timing. There is no doubt that Satoshi's 2008 paper was ground-breaking, yet had it come a decade earlier, no one would have paid any attention to it. As a matter of fact, crypto payments had already been invented by the time Satoshi wrote his paper. In 1983 the cryptographer David Chaum had noticed the insecurity of card payments, especially over the internet. He wrote a paper (1983) describing an early form of encrypted crypto currency that would make internet payments anonymous and safe. He called it electronic cash or e-cash: it was a software the user installed on the PC. Money was stored in that software, but you still needed to have a bank to guarantee the money's authenticity and ensure it wasn't spent twice. It did so by a cryptographic signature. In many ways e-cash worked similarly to PayPal: money was withdrawn from a bank account or credit card and a credit note was given to the retailer as a guarantee. In any case the retailer needed to

Breakthrough-inventors need one thing above all else: the right timing.

have a bank account to which the e-cash could be converted to 'real' money. You can also compare it to a prepaid card, only with an attached virtual wallet where a digital representation of money could be stored. So back in 1983 we had the exchange of fiat money to a digital token that was transferred anonymously, securely and quickly. Sound familiar? Sure, blockchain works with a different verification mechanism, but the benefits offered to the user were pretty much the same.

So why then did DigiCash, Chaum's company, have to file for chapter 11 bankruptcy in 1998, just two years after he left it? It was not that Chaum was a bad entrepreneur. All the big boys such as Citi or Microsoft sat at the table with him. The maker of Windows at one point even offered to pay him US $180 million to put the program on to every PC. So surely he must have had a bad sales strategy, failed to have convinced crucial partners, or made some other game-changing blunder? None of the above. Deutsche Bank, Credit Suisse and Bank Austria were just some of the banks that partnered with him and actively offered e-cash to its customers. Banks had realized the technology's potential and they tested it as an additional option for internet payments. Despite these major partnerships the technology did not take off – end customers just were not interested.

David Chaum and his pioneering ideas went a long way, but he was decades too early. He might have been the first, but, sadly for him, his ideas came too soon and he failed to gain the same recognition as Satoshi Nakamoto, or to inspire a host of TechCrunch articles.

Bitcoin has risen despite – and some would say because of – the fact that it was not another layer on top of the current banking structure. But is adding block after block on a distributed ledger really what made bitcoin succeed and e-cash fail? For bitcoin's first users that might have been the case. The ability to completely bypass the established banking system fits bitcoin's association with the dark side of the web. But this is not what has turned crypto currencies and the blockchain into hype. The world has changed dramatically since 1983. Back then, purchasing on the internet was only done by the most reckless daredevils. Payments were very much cash dominated, particularly outside of the United States. Today, credit, debit and prepaid cards account for a total yearly transaction volume of US $31.878 trillion (The Nilson Report, 2017b). Online banking is displacing bank branches, and by 2022 bank-branch traffic is expected to decline by 36 per cent (Peachey, 2017). ATMs, laptops and mobile phones are all you need to get the job done. When was the last time you visited a branch of your retail bank? In addition, payment terminals are now ubiquitous. The figure for newly shipped terminals amounted to 54.2 million in 2016, an increase of more than 10 million from the previous year (The Nilson Report, 2017a). PayPal has already become the largest online payment method in the United States and covers over US $354 billion in payment volume globally. It has almost 200 million active user accounts (Statista, 2017). Mobile payment is on the rise: in the years between 2017 and 2022 a rise of 132 per cent is forecast for mobile transactions (Pilcher, 2017). The point is, the average person is used to digital tokens of value. Purchase decisions are sometimes made on the method and ease of payment; a shop that does not offer credit-card payments might be shunned. Studies show that each business not offering card payments misses out on $7,000 in revenue each year (Intuit, 2012).

People have also become more impatient. Have you ever stood in a queue at a cash register, dreaming about kicking the terminal to speed up the processing? Contactless cards have increased our expectations even more, as not having to punch in PIN codes for small transactions makes queues faster. We don't have to slide a plastic card into a terminal any more, but can just tap it. So contactless has fuelled the rise of many other payment-form factors, whether that is putting your NFC chip (near-field communication) into a piece of plastic, a contactless sticker, or even a plush mascot. We have come a long way from copper and paper, and even plastic. Everyone understands that money is not driven by a truck from one bank to another if you tap your Mastercard at a terminal. The idea of digital ledgers being updated in the background has taken root, as has the idea of cryptography and data security. Computer and internet penetration are at an all-time high: 51.7 per cent of the world's population have internet access – in Europe it is 80.2 per cent and in the United States it is 88.1 per cent (Internet World Stats, 2017). What's more important, e-commerce has had an impressive winning streak capturing 8.7 per cent of all retail spending, and is set to see double-digit growth until 2020, if you believe market research experts (eMarketer 2016). Unlike three decades ago, the stage is set for an easy, secure and cheap payment system that spans the globe.

Banks also now have higher incentives; as we noted in the last chapter, slashing credit-card fraud alone would save financial institutions almost US $23 billion a year. That is not all though, as there is an even bigger threat knocking on the banks' doors: independent fintechs. To understand the magnitude of the threat posed by the fintechs, we need to look at the history of payments in the recent past. As payment processes have evolved, new functionality has been added, and the payments chain has lengthened. For every step in the chain, a new type of actor appeared, selling services for the small step in the payment process. This enabled these actors to gain expertise and scale advantages to carve out extremely profitable niches spanning the globe. These actors were not independents, but bank subsidiaries or partners. In banking this situation is referred to as 'co-opetition'. Due to the high market concentration, makers of components of the payment value chain competed and cooperated with each other at the same time. Payment instruments only work if customers know they will be able to use their card in every store, or that they will not have to open a bank account with a specific bank to pay their electricity bill. Thus, networks, issuers and acquirers had no choice but to partner with their competitors to build a joint infrastructure. Sometimes this took decades and, due to the complexity and the interdependence of the steps, banks had to find a modus vivendi with each other, while at the same time fighting for customers. This is a major reason for the scale and static structure of the industry today and also explains the comfortable position incumbents are in. At the same time, however, co-opetition made them vulnerable to today's digital competitors (McKinsey, 2017). Blockchain fintechs cannot make banks obsolete, but they can compete for profits without using their infrastructure. This is what makes them different to non-blockchain fintechs that cannot bypass the infrastructure. While in the 1980s the customer interface was a prerogative of banks, today's young start-ups are occupying exactly that.

Blockchain-fintechs can compete for profits without using the infrastructure of banks.

Let's return to pioneers and settlers. Today's blockchain companies are not hopeless adventurers. Some of them are pioneers, others will prove to be settlers, but all of them operate in a much less hostile environment than e-cash. Those who survive will not do so because they have slaughtered incumbents and tried to take their land, but they have infected their minds with an idea and sold them the tools to make it a reality. For Chaum the time was not right, but there was another reason why he failed: he underestimated the power of the natives in the banking sector. He failed to sign a major deal because he thumbed his nose at Microsoft when it offered him US $180 million and the chance to capture the world's computer market overnight. Smart settlers, even though they might feel superior, know when to grit their teeth and give in; they have to understand their weaknesses and the long-term potential of partnerships.

Disrupting the disruptor – how the blockchain itself might become obsolete

The many authors and self-proclaimed experts who write enthusiastically about the benefits of the blockchain often fail to acknowledge its weaknesses. So far for blockchains we have looked at two major obstacles barring it from dominating the market: scalability and energy consumption. In Chapter 2, we will look at how a different technological set-up could remedy these shortcomings. Other roadblocks, however, can only be removed by the passage of time. Even outspoken blockchain supporters (eg Tapscott and Tapscott, 2016) admit the technology is not yet ready for prime time. Amongst other constraints, they say, it lacks 'the *transactional capacity*', meaning that bugs and system failure would be likely if it were suddenly deployed on a large-scale basis. The infrastructure is not ready either; cryptocurrencies' liquidity is insufficient to handle a great surge of users – and, without the crazed money-printers from Satoshi's nightmares, it will stay like this for a long time. In the case of bitcoin, forever. By default, the minting mechanism slows down and screeches to a halt somewhere around the year 2140.

Another potential problem in need of fixing is that user interfaces are currently not very consumer friendly, and new and better wallets still need to be developed. A lack of awareness of where to get and how to use digital currencies, as well as the complexity surrounding crypto security issues are also preventing the technology from going mainstream. For most of the current blockchains, users need private keys to access their money, and keeping them secure is critical because the entire technology relies on public key cryptography. This is one of the major operational risks, because once a user forgets or loses their key, the value they own on the blockchain can never be recovered. There is no password-reset mechanism (Peters, Chapelle and Panayi, 2014), nor can account ownership be proven by an ID card or a fingerprint; knowing the right key is the only proof of ownership. We are not talking about a four-digit PIN-code here; losing the key is actually a very likely scenario given that the code is a 32-character alphanumeric public address. There are other potential issues, for example, if you discover the key has been stolen, there is currently no means to block the money. Nor is it possible to change the key; you would have to create a new account and transfer all your money to get a new password. Moreover, people have not yet formed workable habits to secure their digital possessions. Would you remember to continuously back up your financial data on an external hard drive? How many times have you used the password reset function for passwords? Compared to other challenges, these are issues that can be solved rather easily. Companies such as Circle Internet Financial and Xapo are already developing user-friendly wallets, where typing in the 32-character key is not necessary for every transaction. These firms are looking to dominate the front-end by an easy-to-use and intuitive interface.

Consumers might also struggle when it comes to working out the value of a new currency such as bitcoin, and it will take a significant change in mindset for them to be able to do so with any sense of ease. Could you tell off the cuff whether 0.2267 bitcoins for a bike is a good deal or not? Bitcoin is denominated up to eight decimal points, so even the best mathematicians will need a calculator. It is likely that before readily understanding bitcoin's value most customers will, for quite some time, need to convert everything to dollars, euros, or any other currency they know.

Privacy is another hot topic, despite the pseudonymity. It is possible – but only with a great deal of serious effort – to discover the real identities beneath each pseudonym. In

Chapter 2 we will look at the Silk Road case, which proved this to be true. This idea is not only frightening for bitcoin users, but it also clashes with current regulation. In the European Union every citizen has the right to be forgotten. The European Commission has legislated in the General Data Privacy Regulation that everyone has the right to have their history deleted from the internet (European Commission, nd). But once your name appears on the immutable ledger of a permissionless blockchain, it will be up there forever. Even if transactions are reversed, they still can be seen. Pressed for solutions, blockchain enthusiasts appear at a loss to explain a possible way out of this dilemma. Tapscott and Tapscott (2016) argue that this right should not apply to companies, because they 'have responsibilities that accompany their license to operate'. This level of transparency is, however, rather idealistic, and would undermine the entire dealings of private firms. It would mean that companies could track each transaction of their competitors, suppliers and clients. Chaos would ensue. Besides, it would never be possible to use the bitcoin network just for companies, as they also interact with private citizens for whom the right to be forgotten cannot be waived.

The most serious threat to blockchain technology, however, is not to be found in its own shortcomings, but in another groundbreaking technology: quantum computing. Current digital computing works with transistors and the binary opposition 0-1. Every shred of data has to be encoded as zero or one. The result of the coding is what we know as a bit. Quantum computing, on the other hand, relies on so-called quantum-bits or qubits, which consist of much more information than bits. By using quantum mechanics, the quantum-bit does not need to be encoded as a zero or a one, it can be in both states at the same time. Sounds impressive? It is. But it is equally frightening. This new breed of computers will offer unprecedented computation speed

Quantum computing could easily break crypto codes.

and will not only threaten the blockchain, but the world's entire cryptographic infrastructure. By being able to perform extremely rapid trial-and-error mechanisms it could easily break crypto codes (Franco, 2014). A big black swan. As we discussed in the Introduction, asymmetric cryptography or PKI are the ground on which every widely used form of encrypted communication is built. Smart cards, digitally signed e-mails, VPNs, firewalls – you name it. All of it is at stake with quantum technology.

Let's imagine the worst-case scenario can be averted and governments manage to impose regulation that forbids deciphering PKI communication. Let's also imagine they manage to do so before rogue programmers get hold of the new tools. Let's go even further and imagine control and monitoring mechanisms are put in place on time. This is a scenario with a lot of ifs, but consider this: even after this sequence of events quantum computers could *still* break cryptocurrencies. At least those that work with the proof-of-work mechanism. With super-computers at hand, minting new bitcoins will be so easy that the entire system might collapse. Of course the playing field would be levelled if all miners would get hold of quantum computers, but the first ones to afford them could wreak havoc by altering the previous ledger and imposing their version of the truth of history. A centralized authority could offset this looming threat, but the very idea of it would cause most blockchain fanatics to wince. If you have a limited network of nodes, controlled by one entity, the new computer generation might indeed cause a quantum leap. All nodes could be upgraded simultaneously and selfish motives ruled out.

Still not a new internet

However you feel about the blockchain – enthusiastic about its capabilities or nervous about the things that have not yet been worked out – you probably agree that it will have a significant impact on society and the economy. You would not have bought this book otherwise. Try this experiment: can you think of a suitable adjective that, for you, describes 'technology' in the context of blockchain? If 'disruptive' comes to mind, you are not alone. There is hardly an article written about blockchain, academic or popular, that does not refer to it as 'disruptive'. So what is meant by disruptive, and just how disruptive is it?

The term 'disruptive technology' was coined by Harvard professor Clay Christensen in his book *The Innovator's Dilemma* (1997). It proved to be an infective concept, and the word has been subject to overuse across the globe ever since. Scribes and management gurus have feasted on the sensationalist idea of existing structures being unhinged, whilst there is hardly an industry for which doom-mongers have not predicted rocky waters ahead. However, predicting whether a technology will be disruptive is difficult, almost impossible. Blockchain is a very recent phenomenon and, despite the hype, so far incumbents are not floundering; they have not even started to feel their dominant positions slip away (apart from in the headlines, that is). To foresee whether a new technology will disrupt the existing order, you need to predict two things: the performance dimensions that will be important to the market in the future and how well the new technology will be able to fulfil them (Danneels, 2004). Unfortunately, this is as close as Christensen's ground-breaking work gets to defining what he means by disruptive innovation. This lack of rigidness might be exactly what gave the concept its huge popularity, but it is also responsible for the proliferation of writings ever since.

There are many different interpretations of the word 'disruption'; most of them implicitly drawing a distinction between competence-enhancing and competence-destroying technologies (Tushman and Anderson, 1986). Disruptive technologies, like the blockchain, are in the latter category. They destroy or make obsolete the incumbents' investments. The general line of thinking is that new firms introduce this kind of technology, while incumbent firms work on competence-enhancing technologies – usually meaning faster and more efficient ways to do what they have always been doing, say a laptop producer giving away a larger hard drive for the same price. Incumbent firms are seen as tweaking existing, but moribund, technology. That this is not true for the blockchain, nor for the better part of history, we will see in Chapter 4.

So I define a technology as disruptive when it alters the lines along which firms compete and create a competitive advantage (Danneels, 2004). Consequently, whether the blockchain is a disruptive technology depends on the area within which it is employed. Let's use monetary transactions as an example to illustrate this. To date, the only real performance metric determining whether someone opened up an account in a particular bank has been accessibility, and the geographic proximity of branches used to be a deciding factor. Parents would influence the decision by taking their children to their local branch to open their first bank account. The kids would not tend to question it, or look into the terms and conditions of different banks; all they want is an account to access the salary for their summer job. Once this first step has been taken, it usually leads to a savings account, a debit card, a mortgage, a consumer loan, a credit card, and maybe even an investment product or two, all at the same bank. Human sluggishness is so powerful that it is rare for anyone to have more than one provider for these services. According to the US government, fewer than 50 per cent of people ask for more than one quote when getting a mortgage for their house – perhaps the biggest investment of their lives (Kulaev, 2015). Despite the rise of the internet and easy-to-use comparison sites, the differences between the offers are often so marginal that customers cannot be bothered with the hassle of shopping around.

Often, however, customers do not have a choice, say if they live in a remote place with only one service provider or the platform they are using is mandating to work with a particular company. International payments with Airbnb, for instance, must go through Western Union. If you are reliant on using particular money transfer systems, bad luck. Either you accept their fees and conditions or you will not move your money around the globe. In many regions such as the Philippines, there are particularly few traditional providers of international money transfers (Tapscott and Tapscott, 2016). Ironically, these are often the markets that depend most on remittances sent by diasporas. In these regions the mere existence of blockchain offerings will bring a host of new dimensions to compete on, and those currently monopolizing the markets will suddenly have to care about costs and the service level they are offering.

In the West, blockchain can crimp costs and processing time so significantly that the gap in the offerings may get customers' attention. There is also its enhanced security and the fact that it is tamper proof. Security alone, however, will not allow blockchain to gain competitive advantage. In order for banks to keep their licence to operate, they must vouch for the security of their customers' money. Theoretically, as a customer I don't have to pay heed to how my bank secures its database or even to whether someone hacks my account. Competing on security only makes sense in the business to business (B2B) realm, when banks choose their backend provider, but the backend is not the place where blockchain proponents want to languish.

So blockchain brings different attributes to the table, and the potential to disrupt is certainly there. But what about its – admittedly short – track record? Can we draw parallels to other disruptive innovations? We can. The blockchain exhibits typical features of a disruptive technology in its infancy stage. In the beginning, disruptive technologies lag behind the established ones in serving the mainstream market, as normally the products based on the new technology only appeal to a niche segment and the performance dimensions on which the disruptor's products excel do not meet the purchasing criteria of the mainstream market. Hence incumbent firms focus their resources on tweaking their existing technology (Danneels, 2004). Bitcoin users today have a natural attraction to crypto value, and to risk. Many use blockchains not because of their payment capability but as an investment, and in doing so they enjoy the bitcoin rollercoaster ride. Others still do it for its pseudonymity – unfortunately, even today bitcoin is driven largely by illicit actions. But regardless of their motives, all of the users invest a lot of time to research products, currencies and the mechanisms behind the technology. The mass market is not ready to do the same.

So blockchain's trajectory thus far does indeed resemble other ground-breaking technology in the past. Yet solely being a disruptive, competence-destroying innovation doesn't cut it. For blockchain proponents its significance cannot be overstated, and *paradigm* is another term commonly tossed around in relation to its importance. This is an easy assertion to make, but is there any truth in it? Let's look at the evidence. So-called techno-economic paradigms were first defined in 1982 by an English economist by the name of Christopher Freeman (1982, 1987; Freeman and Perez, 1988). Freeman meticulously analysed influential technical changes throughout human history and proposed a taxonomy that culminates in the techno-economic paradigm. He distinguishes four categories of progress:

- incremental innovation;
- radical innovation;
- changes in technology systems;
- changes in the techno-economic paradigm.

These categories differ in their intensity and impact on economies and markets. Eventually, they determine which strategies firms need to select in order to compete successfully. It is crucial to understand whether the blockchain really represents a paradigmatic shift or another level in the taxonomy.

Incremental innovation is the simplest form of progress. It tweaks processes of the current paradigm, but it is not a game-changer. All it does is make current processes more efficient. While in the beginning of a new paradigm incremental innovation usually makes a huge impact, it slows down with every other round of fine-tuning. In order for the new paradigm to emerge, it takes a series of radical innovations. Powerful radical innovation at the same time can also represent the infrastructure of the new paradigm. The internet is the best example. Besides being an infrastructure that enabled the rise of the digital paradigm, the internet was a radical innovation that fuelled the emergence of a host of adjacent, interrelated industries. By the same token, the blockchain can be defined as radical innovation. It has sparked the emergence of numerous industries such as blockchain (app) development and blockchain consulting, to name but a few. Together these industries build technology systems, which are the components of a technological revolution. They overlap. They impact markets for each other. Above all, they determine the route of future innovation (Perez, 2009).

So how is the blockchain different from previous fintech innovation? After all, there has been innovation in the payment sector claiming to take finance into the digital world. PayPal is the best example of this. Founded only in 1998, its market valuation surpassed that of American Express, one of the giants who pioneered the credit-card business. The most striking thing is not that it displaces an internet payments firm and outdoes an incumbent in terms of value, but that it does so while its earnings and revenue are just a fraction of its competitor (*The Economist,* 2017). This shows investors' expectations. They believe that PayPal has a bright future in the Digital Age. So does that mean it is a technology system in Freeman's model? It does not. PayPal represents neither a new currency nor a new payment system, but builds on existing infrastructure. It does not spark the rise of other industries, nor does it have any noteworthy influence on future technological development. There is no radical innovation. The same is true for Apple Pay and Google Wallet. They all still need users' bank accounts and credit cards and they just provide a new interface while working with established systems in the background. In this respect, the blockchain is much more significant as it does not build on a current payment infrastructure and it holds the potential to influence many industries beyond payment and transactions. Hence, though it does not qualify as a technological revolution or paradigm, it does deserve the label of radical innovation and it gives rise to technological systems. For incumbents the implications are clear: they need to react more strongly than they did to PayPal or Apple Pay.

With the help of such infrastructures and radical innovation, new technologies diffuse and the techno-economic paradigm unfolds, altering the economy and even socio-institutional structures. The more technologies exist within a paradigm, the larger and faster its impact. A series of radical breakthroughs can cluster together and result in interdependent technologies. Take the most recent, ongoing transition: it started around microprocessors, continued with personal computers, software, telecoms and the internet, with each opening their own system trajectory. Each of those radical innovations opened up carrier branches and new infrastructures that make up the technological revolution (Perez, 2009). These are transporting or handling the most crucial resource of this age: data. Data has replaced oil as the world's most precious commodity. The BPs and Shells no longer top the revenue and market capitalizations charts – they have been replaced by the Googles and Amazons. The world's five most valuable firms are data collectors (Kiesnoski, 2017). Blockchain can thus be seen as an infrastructure. It enables the Digital Revolution to reach even more industries, just like the internet or mailing systems did, or as transportation roads did in the Mass-Production Revolution. While the banking sector has changed along the lines of electronic ledgers or e-banking, the underlying paper-based logic has persisted up to this day (Ali *et al*, 2014). The blockchain can push banking through the digital transformation. Ergo, it can never be a paradigm on its own, but a technology system carrying the current digital paradigm; as a carrier branch it brings digitalization to banking. It is a prime example of a catalyst.

Radical breakthroughs are one driver of the expansion of a techno-economic paradigm. The relative cost structure is another (Perez, 2009). One of blockchain's major promises is to slash costs for banks – US $15–20 billion a year from 2022 to be precise (Santander Inno Ventures, Oliver Wyman and Anthemis, 2015). Just as cheap water was the key input to fuel the rise of the Industrial Revolution, the blockchain offers the key input of *cheap trust*, meaning that most of the overhead currently used for eliminating the double-spent problem becomes obsolete. Oil is useless without refineries. Data is useless without trust. The blockchain-enabled trust fulfils all criteria of a technological revolution's key input, among which are inexhaustibility, all-pervasiveness of application, and increasing power with decreasing costs (Perez, 2009). With the set-up of most current blockchains trust is still not cheap, but as we will see in Chapter 2, centralizing blockchains would be able to get it there very soon.

> *The blockchain offers the key input of* cheap trust.

Some of the more modest commentators do not see the blockchain as a paradigm, but of these, many (eg Swan, 2015) do claim it to be the second internet, equal in significance to the first one. Both are radical innovations, and disruptive. These commentators point to the parallel investment levels to back up their assertions, and indeed, with venture capital approaching US $350 million in 2014, and almost $1 billion in 2015, we are talking similar amounts to those shortly after the creation of the internet (Skinner, 2016). Yet this parallel alone is misleading. Bear in mind the trajectory of the digital paradigm: the earlier innovations come, the more difficult it is for them to raise capital. Also, for early innovations the time to market is longer. The more the paradigm takes hold, the easier it becomes to convince investors, find skilled employees and use existing infrastructure. This explains why, despite similar investment levels, the significance of the blockchain's rise cannot be compared to that of the internet. Each techno-economic paradigm at one point becomes dominant and unquestioned, biasing the context towards it (Perez, 2009). The blockchain operates in the already established digital paradigm. This is a difference in heft, but there is also a fundamental one in kind. The internet rose to the most impactful innovation of the digital paradigm because it was open. Every node can change the system. This resulted in the explosion of content, which pulled even more users to it and eventually spiralled towards infinity. The blockchain will always demand consensus, regardless of whether you limit or open the number of nodes. This is the very nature of a trust machine, but it will render networks rigid and hamper the penetration. It is not correct to call it the 'internet of money'. The network is open, but nodes can only act collectively. Even worse: they can only act *as a whole*. Nodes do not have the creative power they have in the internet, but solely the destructive role of denying or granting consensus. So the blockchain is by design different to the internet. The implications for network designers are simple: make it as efficient as possible, not as open as possible. Only once companies grasp this, can they unlock blockchains' true potential. Unfortunately, they are up against a firewall of advocates of the internet-parallel.

CHAPTER TWO

A Libertarian Fantasy in the Most Regulated of Industries

Myth: 'Open blockchains rather than closed ones will power tomorrow's economy.'

A political battle fought in a technical arena

In September 2017 Jamie Dimon (who we first came across in the Introduction) shook the blockchain community once again, but this time with an unprecedented negative outburst. He declared bitcoin to have no future, to be a 'fraud' and 'worse than tulip bulbs'. Any employee trading bitcoin, in his opinion, deserved to be fired for being 'stupid' (Son, Levitt and Louis, 2017). At the same time China banned ICOs, declared bitcoin transactions illegal, shut down bitcoin exchanges and blocked its citizens from using foreign exchanges. China's Great Firewall blocked not only commercial, but also peer-to-peer trades. Financial speculation in the market had become a liability; some traders were even betting against the yuan. China's measures sent the bitcoin price temporarily down by 40 per cent and exposed the currency's serious vulnerabilities. But did the actions of the Chinese government enrage bitcoin fanatics more than Dimon's statement? It surely should have done, but it didn't. Dimon's comment caused a visceral reaction; disgust rose to the surface, particularly in the realm of unfiltered social media. Doomsayers proclaimed bitcoin was about to deal the deathblow to banking, and a host of charges against JP Morgan Chase and Dimon himself popped up on my LinkedIn wall around this time. The tsunami did not abate for days.

This outburst is symptomatic of a deep ideological rift at the centre of the blockchain controversy. In one corner are the incumbents of the banking and payments world, in the other an unusual alliance of crypto evangelists, anarcho-libertarians, entrepreneurs and fraudsters who are set for disruption. In most areas of technological change similar tensions exist, but with blockchain the ideological divides seem intractable. Anti-banking fanatics who most often come from the left of the political centre see the financial institutions – and governments – as rigged. In their view the entire system is built in a way that exploits everyone who is not part of the greedy elite. This rhetoric, however, is now somewhat trite, so the fanatics have turned their objection from an ideological to a technical one: open up transaction verification, or shut them under someone's control.

Dimon was not demonizing the blockchain. He did not speak about JP Morgan Chase abandoning its blockchain initiatives. All he said was that bitcoin will not be the application that will change the financial world; you don't have to be a rocket scientist to reach this conclusion. The energy consumption is unsustainable, the necessary scale unreachable, the usability a pain, and regulation a thing to be bypassed by design. Is it any wonder, then, that many practitioners dismiss it altogether? There is another side of the story, however, and one that is seldom told. It would, in fact, actually be possible to maintain the agility and robustness of distributed ledgers without having the burden of tens of thousands of nodes.

Let me explain how this would work. Two major blockchain set-ups exist: one is centralized (or 'closed') and the other decentralized ('open'). I admit it is confusing to talk about distributed ledger technology that is centralized. But distributed and decentralized are different things. In a distributed system multiple nodes exist that maintain the ledger – the very nature of blockchain. Decentralized, on the other hand, means that *no node has privilege* over the others by the algorithm. Ergo, there can also be a distributed blockchain system where some nodes are given more weight than others – those are centralized, but still distributed blockchains.[1] Bitcoin is a decentralized blockchain where everyone can participate in verifying transactions and each node carries the same heft. Only chosen nodes can vote on the truth. Sometimes commentators confuse the distinction of private versus public blockchains with the juxtaposition of centralized versus decentralized blockchains. In most cases these private and centralized blockchains overlap and vice versa but, strictly speaking, centralized only means that the verification nodes are determined by a central authority. The blockchain owner decides how many and which devices split the entire decision power among them. Public versus private defines whether there are restrictions of who can read and submit transactions for verification (Peters and Panayi, 2015).

So why is the distinction between centralized and decentralized so important? What difference does it make if I have 10 predefined verification nodes, or 10,000 with their numbers growing every day? How does it fit into the ideological war? Centralized blockchains can address many of the weaknesses associated with the currently dominant decentralized applications. One of those weaknesses is the low latency, meaning that the clearing and settlement of transactions takes far too long. The average confirmation time with bitcoin is 10 minutes, which makes it impossible to use it for things such as asset trading, or indeed for payments of any significance. Seeking consensus from thousands of unknown nodes simply does not scale. Sealed-off blockchains, on the other hand, have latency times of seconds. Energy consumption is also more efficient as you no longer need armies of miners burning through gigawatts to create trust. Centralized blockchains are so much faster and more energy efficient because, in the beginning, nodes that are trusted are privileged so you don't need to create trust in a network of unknown nodes by mechanisms such as proof-of-work. At the same time, centralized blockchains give the owner flexibility; they let you rewrite the rules of the system. They also reduce the likelihood of a hostile takeover attack, since the bank knows all decision-making nodes and has all of them under its control.

Keeping control over the nodes has a legal advantage too, as the owners can implement whatever identity checks they want. This is mandatory for every banking licence holder. To satisfy the know-your-customer (KYC) requirement, pseudonymity must be restrained and participants' identities verified. KYC makes it mandatory for banks to know the real, not just digital, identities of transacting parties in an attempt to help combat money laundering and other illegal activities. The prevention of terrorism is a driving force behind KYC, so in the United States the legislation was particularly tightened after the 9/11 attacks – with the US Patriot Act in 2001. Having absolute control over the nodes is also necessary for the right to be forgotten, because only then can you ensure that more than 50 per cent of the network will vote to replace previous transactions. Moreover, transactions on a decentralized blockchain are de facto irreversible, while on a centralized one the history of the ledger can be changed more easily. When you consider the number of mistakes or fraudulent activities that happen on a daily basis, this feature ought to be well received.

Centralized blockchains as the silver-bullet solution

We may want to ask a more general question: do we need any cryptocurrency at all to harness the potential of blockchain technology, or can it be used to power fiat currencies? It depends on the purpose. One area where bitcoin and other cryptocurrencies offer a better solution than fiat currencies is micropayments. Each bitcoin is divisible to eight decimal places, enabling micropayments that are not possible with regular currencies. But for the vast majority of cases, dollars or euros could be transferred via the blockchain just as well as bitcoin. Of course, in the background there would be some crypto token linked to the fiat money, but customers would not need to know about it. All currency and speculation risks would be linked to the 'real' currencies that are managed by central banks. Even more importantly, the acceptance network would be given. Right now neither bitcoin nor any altcoin can be used in stores, apart from the deep web and a handful of pilot projects. It will always be easier to spend pounds than bitcoin. Needless to say, Satoshi Nakamoto's followers are incensed by this idea, but in Japan alone – Nakamoto's own country – 61 banks are engaging in trials with Ripple that are supposed to slash costs by one-third and ensure international transfers go through the same day. Two leading South Korean banks are also in on it (Nikkei, 2017). Ripple is one of the leading cryptocurrencies and continuously ranks in the top three regarding market capitalization. Unlike bitcoin it can power fiat currencies and it has a centralized set-up, which makes it much more efficient and controllable.

Do we need any cryptocurrency at all to harness the potential of blockchain technology?

Financial institutions are already embracing this silver-bullet solution of combining centralized blockchain technology with state-issued, 'real' currencies. Even though blockchain started as an open-source technology, Bank of America filed for and received 43 blockchain patents. Of the 1,045 blockchain patents filed in total, banks hold one in five. After the blockchain-specific companies they are the largest group of patent holders (Decker and Surane, 2018).

So what do the opponents think of all this? Most blockchain disruptors are up in arms against these 'closed' chains, their argument being that centralized blockchains undermine the idea of the technology's founder, who sought to empower the network and not the privileged few. They regard digitalization as inseparable from open-source. To them, bitcoin is the flagbearer, the incorporation of these principles. This is why Jamie Dimon's comment hit a nerve. Disparaging bitcoin is, in their eyes, worse than disparaging the entire blockchain idea. Incumbents harness its power and regulators still get their way. Worse: they can provide customers with a better product.

Of bitcoin users 44 per cent still claim themselves to be 'libertarian or anarcho-capitalists who favour elimination of the state' (Kharif, 2014). Those more moderate accept nation states, but are weary of institutions and companies. For them, centralized blockchains trigger a déjà-vu moment, transporting them back to when the masses gained access to the internet. It was a time of excitement for open-source ideologists, but instead of data being freely accessible to everyone, today it is hoarded and exploited by ever fewer and more powerful corporations (Tapscott and Tapscott, 2016). Yet their argument has evolved from altruism to doom-mongering. With closed blockchains they predict end-user adoption will be hampered because private blockchains lack network effects, invoking the analogy to the intranet/internet distinction to illustrate their point. Decentralized blockchains are likened to the internet and centralized ones the intranet. Decentralized blockchains are seen as potentially connecting every person on the planet because of their openness, just like the internet (eg Hileman, 2016). Centralized blockchains only connect a limited group of people and are thereby bereft of any game-changing potential. This might be a catchy comparison, but it doesn't work. Blockchain is not a product, but a mechanism in the background. If it is standardized, it can be connected to the financial network just like SWIFT – the opposite of an intranet. Proponents of this view have a problem with managing institutions, but the internet parallel cannot be moulded to convincingly fit their argument.

From priests to payment directives – a short history of the institutional imperative of money

Though the comparison with the internet is flawed, libertarian blockchain enthusiasts all too readily forget one true parallel, namely that even the internet cannot dispense with institutions. Without the administration of institutions such as the Internet Corporation for Assigned Names and Numbers (ICANN), there would be no way to ensure the necessary interoperability. Someone has to make sure that domain names and IP addresses are not given out twice. Other agencies (to a large extent part of the US Department of Commerce) have a say too: the Internet Architecture Board, the Internet Governance Forum, and the Internet Society – and the list goes on.

For money, the inherent need to be regulated is even more pronounced than for a communication medium. In the same way that capital fuels economic growth, it can also enable illegal and amoral activity such as money laundering and terrorism. It can foster shadow economies that suck the lifeblood out of the legitimate system, and its mismanagement can throw the entire world's economy into years and decades of depression, just like in the 1930s. But what exactly is money? Sure, it is the coins and notes we carry. It is the lines in our e-banking accounts. But in the end, most of it is simply an entry in a digital ledger. Only US $5 trillion – that is 6.2 per cent of the money in circulation – has a physical manifestation in coins or bills (Desjardins, 2015). Revelations such as these have led libertarians to conclude that money does not need a government, that all the material possessions in the world are a record of debt, that the exchange of furs or food is equal to paper, and by extension so are digital tokens and cryptocurrencies (Skinner, 2016).

This view is flawed on multiple levels. Institutions are necessary to safeguard the value and the exchangeability of money. If someone owes me 2 pounds of fish, I cannot use it to buy 10 bricks to build my house. I would have to negotiate the value of the fish every time and with everyone. This is barter, and it is full of inefficiencies. What's more, fish does not hold its value. In three days it will start to smell and its value will be gone forever. Money, on the other hand, enables commercial transactions over long distances or periods of time. Its units transcend products, and it is easy to calculate with it. It is very difficult, ideally impossible, to forge. It is no coincidence that rare metals such as gold or silver were widely used as means of payment throughout history, starting in 600 BC close to the Temple of Artemis at Ephesus. It was not just Mediterranean people who came up with money in this form. Around 221 BC the first standardized coin was introduced on the other side of the globe, in China (Ferguson, 2008). These coins all bore symbols of state authority. Whether it was the reigning emperor of Rome or the sovereign in China, it was the regents who monopolized the power of minting coins. In order for money to be possible, this power had to be centralized and money had to be regulated. As the system grew, so did the money managers' power.

Every child knows that the invention of the written word marked one of humanity's key milestones, but the reason why humans first picked up a pen (or hammer and chisel) is less well known. It was not to write down stories or philosophy, but to record business transactions. Around 5000 to 4000 BC in ancient Mesopotamia, clay tokens were used as a primitive form of bookkeeping in which transactions were recorded (Nissen, Damerow and Englund, 1993). This formed the basis for money, though that invention did not develop overnight. A thousand years later, around 3000 BC, Babylonian priests in ancient Sumer invented a currency called the shekel. It was a token that farmers received for contributing their wheat to the temple (Skinner, 2016). Just like the emperors on the coins, the priests were a privileged central authority that managed the money flows, and although people back then did not realize it, the clay tokens would have been worthless without the priests' promise to 'buy them back' for the grain they had deposited.

This promise also meant that clay tokens could be handed over or sold to someone else. Like today, debt was transferable. Furthermore, farmers could take grains from the temple in a loan-like fashion. Interestingly, Hammurabi's Babylonians were already familiar with the concept of interest (charging up to 20 per cent), as well as compound interest (Van de Mieroop, 1992). It is no coincidence that the highly developed ancient civilizations were the first to have such advanced monetary institutions. Money and credit enabled rapid growth and other technological, economic and societal breakthroughs. That is not to say that you could not have civilization without money; money was unknown to the inhabitants of South America. The Incas, for example, used labour as the unit of exchange, and though it is difficult to prove causality, they failed to develop writing, the invention that was triggered by bookkeeping across the Atlantic. While the Incan civilization edged forward, it lacked these catalysts that would make it competitive to its European counterparts. When the Spaniard Francisco Pizarro came with horses and cannon battleships, the Incans did not stand a chance. Pizarro's troops plundered their cities, emptied their goldmines, introduced forced labour and eventually annihilated the once proud Incan empire, all in search of the shiny metals of the new world.

The highly developed ancient civilizations were the first to have advanced monetary institutions.

Losing faith in the intrinsic value of money

The Spanish had diligently dug up hundreds and hundreds of tons of gold and silver, only to ship them back and find that they could not, in fact, be used to buy Europe's riches. They drowned the continent's markets in cheap gold and silver and triggered a dramatic decrease of purchasing power. Inflation was born. The Spanish had to learn the hard way that the metals they thought had an absolute value were worth only as much as others were willing to pay for them. What they had failed to understand was that money was not about some precious metal, but about credit; a misunderstanding that would eventually cost them the hegemony in Europe. The English and the Dutch, two particularly innovation-prone nations in terms of finance, took the lead among Europe's seafaring nations (Ferguson, 2008). Had they had institutions that we know today, say a central bank, the rare metal could have been stored, its circulation capped and the value managed.

The link between money and institutional trust gets even clearer with a later development, namely banknotes. In the 17th century, China became the first nation to introduce pieces of paper without intrinsic value, but which worked as well as coins. The reason: trust in the emperor. All over the world, the connection between money and gold was so strong that, even in Victorian times, the belief persisted that paper had a worth just because it represented and granted access to rare metals. This was the 'gold standard'. In reality, even gold's worth was only sustained by the promise that someone will exchange goods or services for them in the future. The bearer medium is completely irrelevant. Money and credit are trust – they are the belief that your virtual possessions will correspond to real ones.

Money and credit are trust – they are the belief that your virtual possessions will correspond to real ones.

Throughout history, earthly money has continuously been associated with the celestial – whether it was the image of Ishtar on the Shekel or of Athena in ancient Greece. The most powerful currency in history leaves the bearer in no doubt in whom they trust.

Not the FED, but God himself. The motto was adopted to be the national motto of the United States and shows how inextricably the American nation and its currency are linked to the belief in God: without God, there is no United States, and without the United States, the dollar loses its value. The libertarian perception that the financial system is just a record of debt does not allow for this faith component. Barter represents an immediate and complete transaction; bills and bitcoins, on the other hand, cannot work without the belief that the item you get will have a predictable value tomorrow. This is the problem with bitcoin's currency aspirations. If it is not government backed, there is no guarantee that it will be freely tradeable in the future and in that sense it *is* a record of debt.

Why the best technical set-up still cannot obliterate institutions

In the past, institutions around money developed out of a *technical* necessity. Someone simply had to manage the flow of funds. In 16th-century Europe, goldsmiths started to issue IOUs after receiving gold deposits. They, as well as the early banks, had only access to ledgers kept by themselves. Essentially, they lacked an interbank settlement, meaning if their customers wanted to pay a bill they had to check in their IOUs and take the money to the other bank. Then *interbanking* was invented. It allowed banks to transfer money directly to each other. Customers and banks saved time, and it reduced risk as you could not be robbed while transporting your gold from one bank to another. But this initial network consisted only of bilateral agreements. Hence, the *clearing bank* solution was invented, where one bank sits at the centre and clears transactions of the entire network (Goodhart, 1988).

The technical infrastructure demands trust, and this is the part the blockchain can revolutionize – it is the engine for fast and secure transactions, a trust machine. Yet the trust it creates must not be confused with the trust that enables monetary systems.

The blockchain guarantees that all transactions are authentic and that the minting of the cryptocurrency is legitimate. It can combat inflation by limiting the number of currency units in circulation, or be pre-parameterized in any other way a currency issuer wishes. This would mean that rules determining when new currency should be issued could be set in advance. Yet this technical underpinning alone cannot promise there will be someone to buy back your alphanumeric code. It cannot link the currency to the output of an economy. Neither can it grant stability. Financial history has taught us that a lack of institutional control can have devastating consequences. The great depression from 1929 would never have happened had it not been for instability caused by the lack of federal control over banks. The Federal Reserve was only created in 1913 due to fears of governmental overreach. The idea of free banking ensured low entry barriers and capital requirements, and state lines prohibiting the rise of national giants fuelled the need for independent banks in every corner of the United States. Their number skyrocketed from fewer than 12,000 in 1899 to more than 30,000 in 1922. Droves of undercapitalized banks contributed towards the worst financial crisis in US history and the Great Depression (Ferguson, 2008).

The crash revealed not only the financial connectedness of the US economy, but also the global connectedness. Most banks were undercapitalized, and seeking back money they had lent to other institutions had a cataclysmic chain effect. This was highlighted further by the recession triggered by the events of 2007. It made pointedly clear that each monetary system needs a lender of last resort to lend money to banks in crisis and prevent the system from collapsing. The central banks' role in keeping banks liquid is at least as important as the minting of coins and bills and setting monetary policy. It only takes one systemically important player to go bust to put the entire economy in recession for decades. So yes, the blockchain is a game-changing technology that can cut out the intermediary, but there will always be a vital role for regulators to play.

Financial innovation and the link to techno-economic breakthroughs

What these turning points in financial history show is that financial innovation is linked to a broader evolution of a civilization; indeed many historians are still undecided as to which development is the trigger and which the effect.

What is undisputed, though, is that breakthroughs were not isolated. Does a simultaneous revolution in technology, trade and commerce sound familiar? That's right – a paradigm. So it is no wonder that the current digital paradigm is also accompanied by a revolution in finance. Change such as this is always manifested in legislation. In many ways, legislation results from a blend of techno-economic developments: actors, business models and infrastructure adapt to the new paradigm and new rules are needed to reflect those new market realities. Today, regulation is starting to be less protective of incumbents. Take the EU's European Commission's Payment Services Directive 2007 (PSD). It harmonized the payments industry for banks and non-banks with a legal framework. Under 'market rules' it described which companies are allowed to operate as providers of payment services, and under 'business conduct rules' it specified things such as transparency or transaction execution. New technological advances were accounted for in the major revision of the directive (PSD2) that came into effect in January 2018. PSD2 is seminal for other legislatures around the world. It mandates strong customer authentication in online retailing and levels the playing field for non-banks. For instance, banks are now required to provide an application programming interface (API) to third parties, which allows them to initiate transactions and see account data. This enables the integration of much of what fintechs do.

Blockchain is one of those technologies that, by its mere existence, pushes the need for equalizing legislation such as PSD2, whilst at the same time being significantly shaped by it. With PSD2, fintechs will gain access to 1 billion bank accounts due to the mandated opening of APIs. Roland Berger, a consultancy, estimates that this could cost banks up to 40 per cent of the profits in the retail segment (Russo, 2017). New regulation lowers barriers to entry, and a surge in competition will send margins down. Whereas, for customers, financial services become cheaper, for the providers the market attractiveness falls and they have to hunt for new revenue streams and business models. This once again illustrates the need for institutions. Without the regulator setting the frame, blockchain would remain a niche, just like bitcoin. By taking a stance with PSD2, the EU opens the doors for blockchain specialists to become part of the big payment system. It breathes legitimacy into them and pulls them out of the shady part of the economy. Besides a general liberalization trend, the market will also be shaped by specific regulations on decentralized ledgers and cryptocurrencies. In the next section we look at how legislation around cryptocurrencies in New York tilted the scales towards established and large institutions, which can fully utilize their core competencies. Further, it underscores the importance of the regulator in shaping the competitive context. In Chapter 3 we will find out just how strong its grip might be.

Leviathan's strong hand – why regulators might end up picking the technology format

Despite the top ranks of governments and central banks being sprinkled with finance veterans, regulation is not playing into incumbents' hands. It is getting more demanding and more restrictive, especially for 'systemically important' banks; General Electric's exit from banking in 2015 bears witness to this. GE Capital, the name of the spin-off, was the seventh largest bank in the United States and had to be bailed out by the government after the financial crisis. The volatility and risk that GE Capital introduced to the mother company had an adverse effect on share prices. The giant left the arena, selling most of its US retailing business to Goldman.

At the same time, regulation becomes more inclusive of non-banks. The financial crisis triggered in 2008 caused a ripple that is still being felt today, with more stringent regulation making the environment much more hostile for incumbents. Financial actors spend millions of dollars and euros love-bombing the institutions, but their legally privileged position is slowly slipping away. The above-mentioned PSD2 forces banks to open their APIs to competitors. Fintechs can thus easily plug their solutions to banks' interfaces without having to build up the entire infrastructure in order to gain access to the customer.

Financial actors spend millions of dollars and euros love-bombing the institutions, but their legally privileged position is slowly slipping away.

China's powerplay in its regulatory clampdown on bitcoin is an impressive example of regulators' might. In the West, control might take less drastic, but equally effective measures. The PSD2 shows how governments can single-handedly define the competitive frame for payments. But before we look at the way governments in the United States and Europe treat the new technology, the distinction between the blockchain as an underlying technology and specific cryptocurrencies has to be stressed once again.

While there is little legislation on the blockchain, bitcoin has received global attention from regulators. A host of countries including Bangladesh, Bolivia, Ecuador, Kyrgyzstan and Vietnam have banned cryptocurrency altogether. China, though not having a formal bitcoin ban in place, has banned ICOs and exchanges. The environment is hostile. The stance towards bitcoin in the Western world, however, is different. It is not that the legislation is idle but different jurisdictions disagree. In the UK, bitcoin is a currency and thus exempt from VAT, whereas the US taxes it like property; bitcoin is subject to capital gains tax. For matters other than taxation the US regulates bitcoin as a currency (Swan, 2015). For the State of New York, the mere classification of bitcoin was not enough. New York was the 20th-century epicentre of finance, and it wanted to remain so in the 21st century by introducing the concept of BitLicense. To obtain such a licence, companies handling blockchain transactions had to follow a set of complex rules that included capital requirements, adherence to anti-money-laundering (AML) measures, regular audits, and prior approval to changing specifications and mechanisms of their products. The idea was to have a sort of bank licence that ensured end customers enjoyed the same governmental protection as with fiat currencies. Of course such regulation eliminates fraud and money laundering and also encourages people to invest in and use cryptocurrencies. Yet it also skews the chances of being able to use cryptocurrencies towards bigger companies that can use their existing infrastructure, financial resources and compliance know-how. Ergo, instead of attracting brainy entrepreneurs to the Big Apple, a mass exodus of blockchain start-ups was triggered while the established institutions with big budgets stayed. Three years after the introduction, a whacking four companies obtained the licence, and only five have been rejected (Brennan, 2018).

New York's pioneering attempt gives a hint of what regulation holds in store; its success might only come when more jurisdictions apply a similar, but perhaps laxer, licence. In Canada a 'lighter-touch' approach with cryptocurrencies was suggested by the Senate to prevent the technology's potential from being stifled. In order to still comply with anti-money-laundering regulation they issued a mandate that digital currency exchanges (so not all bitcoin companies) meet the same requirements as traditional money businesses (Canadian Senate, 2015). Exchanges are the interface between cryptocurrencies and fiat currencies, where you can change your dollars for bitcoin and vice versa. It will take years of collecting data to determine which of the approaches is more successful, and even then you can expect politicians to argue about regional differences and which solution to choose. The only thing we can be certain of is that bitcoin licences will look increasingly like banking licences.

Blockchain-specific legislation, on the other hand, is scarce. Regulations for moving, storing and lending money are not technology-centric. Regulators set the criteria that need to be met; how those are achieved is mostly down to the financial services providers. So if blockchains are simply used for fiat currencies and don't include crypto value, very little specific legislation would have to be drafted. New laws would be needed, however, if the blockchain were to fundamentally change banking business models. There are rules for payments in general that hint at which technical standard will be tolerated and which not. We will not be looking at country-specific precepts in this book, but there are maxims for banking that apply for most territories. One of those maxims is the aforementioned know-your-customer (KYC) principle. First and foremost, KYC may have a profound impact on whether or not centralized or decentralized blockchains are tolerated, and financial firms will only be able to satisfy requirements with the former. KYC will tilt the format wars in favour of banks.

KYC will tilt the format wars in favour of banks.

But why is KYC at odds with cryptocurrencies in the first place? After all, digital coins work with an openly accessible, immutable ledger in which no transaction can be hidden. At the same time, however, the lack of user identification does not comply with KYC. This confusion exists because of a fundamental distinction that regularly gets blurred: pseudonymity versus anonymity (Brito and Castillo, 2013). Whilst pseudonymity means I can hide behind any fake name, anonymity means that not even this fake name can be seen by others. Bitcoin and other public blockchains offer its users only the former, not the latter. The ledger and its history are publicly accessible, but the identities of the transacting parties are hidden behind pseudonyms. There are no identity requirements in the bitcoin network – people can join without providing names or e-mail addresses, which contrasts with the identity-centric model practised by, for example, credit-card companies. Thanks to the blockchain mechanism the nodes serve in self-interest and thus uphold the system. Trust in others became unnecessary and, with it, the need to know the real identities of the transacting parties.

Yet some critics have suggested that it is, indeed, possible to trace back user pseudonyms to IP addresses participating in bitcoin transactions if they are not protected by special software (Biryukov, Khovratovich and Pustogarov, 2014). We mentioned the infamous Silk Road crackdown briefly in Chapter 1 in relation to privacy and pseudonymity. Ross William Ulbricht, the founder of the Silk Road darknet market, was seized by the FBI in 2013 for trafficking weapons, drugs and child pornography worth US $200 million via the bitcoin blockchain as a payment system. He evaded the authorities for years before the FBI eventually tracked him down (Umeh, 2016).

There are anonymization programs for bitcoins. According to studies (Möser, Böhme and Breuker, 2013) some are more effective than others. Bitcoin Fog and Blockchain.info are two of the better ones, while BitLaundry has been shown to be less convincing. But regardless of whether anonymity can be lifted without additional software protection, it is seen as the major obstacle to bitcoin implementation by banks because it violates their KYC precept. Fortunately, there are ways to solve the KYC dilemma. Providers of wallets and exchanges can require customers to confirm their identity. For example, Coinbase's wallet collects users' IP addresses, device and mobile network information. People's right to be forgotten, on the other hand, is impossible to implement. Again it has to be stressed that if a private or centralized blockchain is used, banks can set the rules and force the participants to disclose their identities, rewrite the ledger, and seal off the transaction history from the public.

Centralized blockchains do not just help to be compliant, they can also help with the reporting. The likes of PSD2 or Basel III demand huge amounts of data, as well as human resources to salvage data from past transactions. This could all be shouldered much more easily if everything was recorded on the immutable and complete blockchain ledger. Instant identity verification would mean fewer costs for bank branches, and it would also help regulators with the reams of heterogenous data that come their way. The Euro Banking Association (2015) sees distributed crypto technologies as a cost-efficient way of achieving compliance to KYC and AML rather than a reason to alter laws. Some direct banks – Fidor is a pioneer – already use the Ripple blockchain to achieve KYC and AML compliance. Again, a centralized set-up is the only reasonable solution, because no bank wants to be completely transparent and hand in all their data to the regulators.

Format wars in full swing

Changing an industry's structure is slow; it is quite rare for breakthrough innovation to come along and trigger a transitional phase, causing companies to compete with each other to get to the top of the food chain. The safest way to get there is to impose your own product design as the dominant one, locking out competitors that do not have the legal rights or technical expertise to offer the standard. Alternatively, you could license its format and achieve superior profitability just as Matsushita did with VHS videos. Losing format wars, on the other hand, is very costly and can put companies out of business. So, are there any signs of such a game changer in the blockchain realm? Regulating authorities favour closed blockchains, yet centralization is not a format, but a technical design decision. A format is a specific blockchain or a set of standardized APIs – something that companies, not regulators, will provide.

For a long time, bitcoin was the flagbearer. But bitcoin has failed to deliver, triggering hundreds of ICOs and a series of banking initiatives. Besides consortia, some banks are developing in-house cryptocurrencies (Citigroup), while others are investing in start-ups (Goldman Sachs) or cooperating with them (Barclays, UBS and the Commonwealth Bank of Australia). They are all hoping to set the industry standard (Wild, Arnold and Stafford, 2015). Centralized blockchains abound. At the same time, however, many fintechs are focusing their efforts on decentralized blockchains, not only threatening to destroy banks' core competencies, but also making their centralized blockchain efforts obsolete. Paradoxically, these fintechs are often funded by those same banks. Put simply, financial companies are diversifying their risk, which is natural in any kind of format war. It does highlight, however, just how uncertain financial companies are about which design or format might end up succeeding.

Financial companies are diversifying their risk, which is natural in any kind of format war.

With so many incumbents and start-ups working on their own solutions, how is any one format going to become dominant? Management theory lists five strategies (Jones and Hill, 2012):

- ensure a supply of complements (eg a supply of games for a video-gaming console);
- license your format to others;
- price and market aggressively;
- leverage a killer application;
- cooperate with competitors.

Banking and finance are very specific in that they demand interoperability among the competitors, which is why, in the past, none of the first three strategies was applied successfully to innovation in payment systems. The aforementioned co-opetition set the pace across the value chain. So cooperation with others and the hunt for a killer application worked best and usually went hand in hand.

Leveraging a killer application often brings a sudden end to the format battle, which makes it all the more important to identify it as early as possible in the transition phase. So how do you spot it? There are two steps: 1) identify the specific product attributes enabled by the new technology; 2) match these attributes with customers' needs (MacMillan and McGrath, 2000).

For most blockchain advocates there is no doubt that bitcoin is this killer application. Bitcoin is by far the best-known cryptocurrency, even much better known than the blockchain itself; in fact, to explain the blockchain most resort to bitcoin (as in the 2016 book title *Blockchain Revolution: How the technology behind bitcoin is changing money, business, and the world* by the Tapscotts). Bitcoin is seeing constant growth and has the highest market capitalization at US $164 billion, followed by Ethereum in second place with $90 billion and Ripple in third at $44 billion (Coinmarketcap, 15 February 2018). Bitcoin is used by many fintechs such as the Goldman Sachs-backed Circle Internet Financial; however, it does not necessarily have the attributes the mass market is demanding. Pseudonymity is not what the average person craves, and fiat currencies are not so battered by inflation that peoples' savings are in freefall. Some rare exceptions exist such as Venezuela, where hyperinflation is so high that the regime has issued a crypto coin called Petro, which is supposedly backed by the country's oil resources. Customers need a large acceptance network, low transaction fees and a speedy payment process. But as we saw earlier, with an average confirmation time of 10 minutes and acceptance points concentrated in the deep web, bitcoin is unable to meet these needs. These facts alone disqualify bitcoin as the killer application, never mind the scale limitations or energy consumption. For those who believe bitcoin is already too big to fail, consider this: despite its clear dominance among blockchains, its market cap stands at US $164 billion in February 2018. That is a drop in the ocean compared to the world's total monetary value of $80.9 trillion (Desjardins, 2015). At the time of writing, in 2018, there are 1,530 active altcoins (altcoins are basically alternative cryptocurrencies, ie all crypto coins except bitcoin) (Coinmarketcap, 15 February 2018). Some are scams, some ventures by trustworthy institutions, but most of them predict that bitcoin will not be the leading cryptocurrency in the future.

It may be that the killer application will not be one coin or one particular token, but the technology facilitating communication between applications, the so-called interledger technology. In the list of crypto coins with the highest market capitalization, second and third place go to two such aspirants: Ripple and Ethereum. Ripple's real innovation is not its coin (XRP), but its protocol, RippleNet, which can be used by banks as an addition – or even a replacement – to the SWIFT network. For the Ripple token it is irrelevant whether a cryptocurrency such as bitcoin or dollars and euros are transferred. Ripple links the old system with the new ones by simply offering an API that every bank can use. This interledger solution ties together different payment systems, enabling banks to transfer funds without any intermediary, thus saving cost and time. Ethereum is another big application that facilitates large-scale interoperability. It is a development platform and a programming language that enables new applications to be built. But the real game changer is that it is 'Turing complete', which means it can run any coin, any blockchain, any protocol, no matter what the platform and application. What's more, it can be used to create smart contracts that are connected to multiple blockchains (Swan, 2015).

Both Ripple and Ethereum are extremely powerful platforms that seek to underpin the new payment system, and it is much more likely that one of them will lead the way than bitcoin or any other specific cryptocurrency. For scalability reasons, Ripple would seem to be even better placed than Ethereum. Bitcoin can do 16 transactions per second, Ethereum 15, and Ripple 1,500. While the average transaction time for bitcoin is more than an hour, for Ripple it is four seconds, according to their website. Sure, bitcoin's speed can be improved, but if the gap is so exorbitant to begin with, it is difficult to believe that it could ever be closed.

So incumbents are right to work on centralized blockchains. But what about smaller players that do not have the necessary heft to force a format over the industry? An option would be just to wait and try to be the quickest emulator, but building a large-scale blockchain project takes too much time; it cannot be done overnight. Besides, the advantages of being the quickest mover are usually short-lived. To gain advantage, smaller players should consider joint ventures, acquisitions, alliances or licences; these are all ways in which companies can insource missing expertise. Most of the big organizations take part in some form of cooperation, often in parallel with their own efforts. It is in the nature of banks to seek interoperability of systems; they have, after all, created unified standards in the past. SWIFT, founded in 1973, the private exchange network on which all interbank messages (ie transfers) currently run on, was one such project. Similar cooperation happened in 1970 when 243 banks got together to create Visa (Deutsche Bank, 2016). The model has proven to be extremely successful, and the banks seem to be replicating it once more with the advent of the blockchain. As mentioned briefly in the Introduction, the R3 CEV Consortium was launched at the end of 2015. This is an industry initiative that is supposed to create a common blockchain standard between banks and harmonize the multitude of closed blockchains. Most of the founders and early members were banking behemoths. BNP Paribas, Goldman Sachs, UBS, Royal Bank of Scotland, Barclays, JP Morgan and Credit Suisse are just some of them. By December 2017 more than 100 leading financial institutions and regulators had joined.

The second big collaboration amongst the world's leading financial institutions was launched months after R3 CEV, namely the Hyperledger Project. This Linux-led initiative included the

R3 CEV consortium as a founding member, together with an impressive roster of financial and technology companies such as JP Morgan, the London Stock Exchange, Accenture, or Cisco, as well as the SWIFT network itself. The Hyperledger project is an open-source effort that has set itself the goal to develop a 'blockchain for business', but they reject bitcoins and the entire system of decentralized blockchains. The idea is to create a standard for the banking industry while limiting the number of nodes.

From a purely technical point of view, centralized blockchains beat decentralized ones. Sure, these closed blockchains are less of a revolution than Nakamoto and his disciples had in mind, and they are not newsworthy enough for excessive media attention. At the end of the day, though, it is neither Nakamoto's followers nor the media who will determine blockchain's future; the end customer will. In the meantime, banks are largely unaffected by the hype and pound their tried-and-tested path of cooperation. Will this be enough?

Neither Nakamoto's followers nor the media will determine blockchain's future; the end-customer will.

Note

1 In the literature you will also find the terminology permissioned/permissionless blockchains, which corresponds to the centralized/decentralized dichotomy. Permissioned blockchains only allow pre-specified verification nodes.

CHAPTER THREE

The Dreaded Kodak Moment that will Never Happen – Why Banking is Different

Myth: 'With the success of the blockchain comes the downfall of the banks.'

Cutting the value chain to size

At the end of 2016, Deloitte, Metro Bank and the distributed ledger technology company SETL issued 100 test debit cards to Deloitte's employees, who used them to buy cupcakes in a trial environment. The smart-card balances on the cards were updated immediately and were completely compliant with KYC and AML regulation. The ledger technology ran multiple chains in parallel, which solved the speed problem associated with cryptocurrency applications such as bitcoin. The employees paid in sterling: fiat currency. SETL technology has two big advantages. First, it can process tens of thousands of transactions per second – equal to the big card networks – and second is its interoperability. Just like a SIM card in a mobile phone, the ledger technology can be used for transactions regardless of the card issuer (Deloitte, 2016).

This pilot gave a glimpse of what a blockchain-enhanced future might look like. Banks are still part of the chain, but intermediaries are not. For a transaction to happen, all you need is a sender, a receiver, a bank and a blockchain company; the latter could even be integrated into the bank. As we have seen, the blockchain's central promise is to eliminate the intermediary by creating trust via algorithms. Even the Euro Banking Association (2015) foresees that the blockchain will reduce the reliance on trusted third parties such as payment providers, insurers, companies pooling risks, etc. Among those most at risk are credit-card companies, money transfer services, acquirers and payment processors. Clearing houses will be affected too, although, according to a report by Citi Group, they 'may modestly suffer' because banks could settle trades themselves (Citi GPS, 2016). Citi's report paints a better outlook for banking institutions, although it does note that all banks will need to share the same blockchain to survive. As we saw in Chapter 2, interledger solutions such as Ripple and consortia such as the R3 CEV that work on unified standards will pave the road to success.

Why are intermediaries at such high risk? The complex process requires a host of groups to make secure payments possible. A central group are payment processors, third parties that handle transactions on behalf of merchants. In each credit- and debit-card transaction, they are responsible for authorization and settlement. They validate the transaction by forwarding it to the issuing bank or credit-card company for verification. Processors are prototypical intermediaries because without them a merchant cannot complete a payment transaction. As such, they are at huge risk from P2P verification mechanisms. Credit-card companies face similar pressures from the blockchain. They provide a payments network and charge the merchants card fees in the range of 1–3 per cent of the transaction value. However, credit-card processors are less at risk than pure processors, partly because they offer other services such as insurance or loyalty programmes, but mainly because the likes of Amex and Visa command globally powerful business to consumer (B2C) brands. However, this is unlikely to help them sustain their position in the long run, so they too are proactively trying to harness the potential of the blockchain. Visa, for example, is working on bitcoin remittance services, while Mastercard and Amex are investing in Abra and the Digital Currency Group, two blockchain startups (Hileman, 2016). Furthermore, Mastercard has filed four blockchain patents to improve settlement systems (Redman, 2016).

Money transfer services (or wire transmittance services) such as Western Union are running the largest risk of obsolescence. The global remittance market is estimated at US $514 billion, with transactions fees reaching rates of 7–30 per cent (*The Economist*, 2012). Many fintechs offer nearly free alternatives to move larger sums of money across country borders and, if banks jump on the blockchain bandwagon, there will be no customer segment left needing wire transmittance services. Their value proposition is to move money across state borders without a bank account – nothing that makes them irreplaceable.

It is not surprising that these challengers have the ability to threaten the core business of long-established players; however, what might be less expected is that they also have the potential to displace the current rising stars. PayPal is one such example. This online payments platform builds on existing payments infrastructure, using bank accounts or credit-card networks. Yet they capture significant profits. PayPal has a yearly revenue of US $13.1 billion (Statista, 2018). However the blockchain could slash not just one, but two layers of intermediaries and put their enterprise on shaky ground. PayPal are painfully aware of this and have reacted by entering into partnerships with Bitpay, Coinbase and GoCoin – three leading payment processors for bitcoins (Mac, 2014). A former CEO of the bitcoin wallet company Xapo has joined PayPal's board of directors (Hileman, 2016).

What about the biggest bunch, the banks? In general, the services of retail banks can be grouped into three major categories: store value (ie accounts or stocks), move value (ie provide a payment and transaction utility), and provide access to value (ie loans). Fintechs proclaiming the end of banks have to prove they can do a better – or at least equally good – job with all three of those functions. This has not yet happened, nor is it likely to happen. Blockchain's claim is first and foremost to revolutionize the movement of money. Banks will not be cut from the value chain; the technology will simply open up the market structure within banking. This might disappoint the doom-mongers, but its significance should not be underestimated. An extensive study (Bikker and Haaf, 2002) about global banking market structures found a very high degree of concentration nationally, with more competition internationally. The concentration is especially strong in Europe, to a large extent as a result of numerous mergers, as well as regulation warding off banks from competition in the past. In most of Europe's countries the market structure is one of 'monopolistic competition'. The US market is somewhat different. Due to the 1933 Banking Act (or Glass–Steagall Act) the United States today has a greater number of smaller-sized community banks than other countries. Of the 5,701 institutions only 0.2 per cent had more than 1,000 branches and only 1.4 per cent had between 100 and 1,000 branches as at the end of 2016 (USBankLocations.com, 2018). Yet even the United States is seeing a trend towards market consolidation, which is partly due to mergers and acquisitions, and partly because small banks are likely to fail. In the United States 85 per cent of all bank failures occur at those institutions that have assets worth less than $1 billion (Government Accountability Office, 2013).

Stability is a very important factor to consider when discussing the banking market structure. Disregarding competitive shifts by mergers, acquisitions or exits, there is very little movement in competitive standing, and small gains in market share are not so much driven by innovation as they are by buying customers. Looking at statistics about which banks won and lost customers (Statista, 2017), it is amazing how static high-street banks' customer portfolios are. In the UK there is extremely reliable data, as the vast majority of customers use the current-account switch service (CASS) to change their bank. In the second quarter of 2017, Nationwide led the statistic with a net gain in new customers of 38,626. The second most successful, TSB, reached 20,120, while HSBC came in third with a mere 4,927. All others were either in equilibrium or had a loss in customers. There is, however, one segment that is growing exponentially: digital banks.

Independent of the blockchain, Citi GPS (2016) forecasts a stark decline in bank branches. Between 2014 and 2025 they are estimated to fall by 33 per cent in the United States and by 45 per cent in the euro area. Whilst the number of bank branches is decreasing, a new breed of banks known as 'direct' or 'digital' banks is on the rise. These digitally led banks focus on basic offerings such as debit cards and savings functionality. They have no branches, but instead operate via mobile integration. With the startup N26, for example, you can open a bank account with an IBAN (International Bank Account Number) within eight minutes completely via phone. More prominent examples include Moven, Simple, GoBank and Bluebird in the United States, as well as Fidor and mBank in Europe. The United States already accounts for more than 20 million active customers and 7 million more, including prepaid card programs. This adds up to a whopping 9 per cent market share (King, 2014). Accenture (2013) estimates that direct banks could grab around 35 per cent market share from full-service banks by 2020.

Digital banks can either be arms of existing institutions or independents; however, many of these independents are not actually independent institutions, and will have affiliations with traditional banks. The world's five largest direct banks are all either arms of or affiliated with a traditional bank; among the top 20 banks, there are 15. The independent banks not affiliated with larger institutions are more often hyped for their innovativeness, but they reach comparably little of the market – German Fidor has a mere 0.2 million customers (Frost and Sullivan, 2016). Besides size, profitability is also on the incumbents' side; in Germany, the internet arm of the Dutch ING is not only the third largest, but one of the most profitable institutions of retail banking as a whole. Digital banks have not been a game changer so far, and although the name might suggest it, they do not actually bring digitalization to banking. All they change is the interaction with the end customer. Services are more convenient and overhead costs are slashed. No doubt this helps to better service a particular target group, yet the back-end is identical to that of bricks-and-mortar banks. So digital banks have not been as significant as they were first forecast to be, but, as with the rest of the value chain, the blockchain is likely to transform things. Current participants will face mounting challenges, especially the non-bank intermediaries, and new and less cooperative players will soon be on the scene.

> *Digital banks have not been as significant as they were first forecast to be, but the blockchain is likely to transform things.*

New sharks in the ocean

Business professors, management gurus and CEOs have one thing in common: their obsession in finding, building and sustaining a competitive edge over firms wrangling for the same customers. This hunt for the competitive advantage is set to become more pronounced as disruptive technological innovation takes hold.

There are four competing paradigms that explain where competitive advantage stems from:

- strategic conflict approach (part of market externalities approach);
- competitive forces approach (part of market externalities approach);
- resource-based perspectives (part of the firm-level approach, see Chapter 5);
- dynamic capabilities (part of the firm-level approach, see Chapter 5).

The first two look at market externalities – mainly competition – and how they are shaped by innovation. The focal point is the market structure and the strategic choices of players, suppliers and customers. The other two groups analyse which companies are best suited to gain the upper hand under new market conditions, arguing that it is not the market situation that makes an industry desirable, but rather the fit to the firm's core competencies (Teece, Pisano and Shuen, 1997). To grasp blockchain's impact we will need to use all four of the competing paradigms. In this chapter, we see how blockchain will alter the market structure. In Chapter 5 we then take a look at the other side of the coin, namely the core competencies needed.

The strategic conflict approach (eg Shapiro, 1989) considers how incumbents can manage competition via strategic investment, information imbalances, pricing and signalling. Signalling includes predatory pricing or limit pricing; it means incumbents set prices extremely low and destroy their margins on purpose, not to serve the customer but to cut so deep into competitors' profitability they leave the arena or don't enter it in the first place. Once the competition is destroyed, the signalling company can then raise its prices again. In strategic conflict, keeping the market position is the highest precept, so it is all about controlling the market environment. These moves require strategic and irreversible commitments in order to be effective.

The problem, however, is that this approach is underpinned by game theory, a concept that has been in vogue in academia for decades and which asks how each actor anticipates the other's reaction to their own decisions. While it can be a good exercise to think through the scenarios that might unfold depending on which route you take, at the end of the day the generated models fail to deliver useful predictions and testable insights (Sutton, 1992). If big power gaps persist between the actors in an industry, the outcomes of the game-theoretical analysis will be correct. But is it really necessary to do it? You don't need a computer model to tell you that if Amazon introduces free shipping, other retailers' hands will be forced to do the same. In balanced-out power relations the model's benefit becomes moot and only helps in industries with little and slow technological change (Teece, Pisano and Shuen, 1997). Hence, the strategic conflict approach provides little support in determining the impact of the blockchain on banking. The competitive forces theory does a better job.

To everyone who earned their salt as a management consultant or sat through even one course at business school, the name Michael Porter will ring a bell. The revered Harvard professor is the most cited author in business and economics (HBS, nd). Back in the 1980s and 1990s he revolutionized corporate thinking about competition by importing concepts from economics into management strategy. No one could translate competitive advantage into bullet points the way he could, and his relevance and importance persists today. Of all his works, the competitive forces model is his most important legacy. The essence of it is that firms should seek out industries that offer high profitability due to weak competition. Once found, they should take action to keep competitive forces down or find calm corners where market forces are the weakest, otherwise their profitability will directly suffer (Teece, Pisano and Shuen, 1997). It is a simple principle: if the number of competitors goes up, profits go down.

The slices of the pie get thinner. To make the approach more practicable Porter (1979, 1980, 1985) broke down the competitive forces to five pillars that have an impact on profitability levels:

- the bargaining power of customers;
- the bargaining power of suppliers;
- the threat of substitute products and services;
- the threat of new entrants;
- rivalry in the industry. (Porter, 1979)

Retail banking has always been an attractive industry according to this model, but as we have seen, industry structures can change through innovation, whereby new technology unfreezes, changes and refreezes them again. This is exactly what the blockchain will do, and here is how.

The first force is the bargaining power of buyers. What currently weakens buyers' power in retail banking is that they are too dispersed; they have no joint lobby. There are no individual customers that drive proportionally high chunks of the revenue as better-off individuals turn to private bankers. Though financial switching costs are low and the customer has the power to unilaterally change the supplier, it hardly ever happens. More often than not, changing banks requires a behavioural change, and one that customers are often not willing to make for the financial benefit they might gain from switching, especially if the products have little emotional significance. Interest rates or credit-card fees do not tend to evoke emotion. All this reduces the buyers' power. In a blockchain-based world, however, switching providers will be easier, there will be a much wider range to choose from, and the new offerings will be better differentiated because an army of fintechs will follow a focus strategy, delivering solutions tailored to the needs of specific customer groups. Costs and offerings will be more transparent and packed into apps.

So while we would only expect to see a slight power shift towards the customers, the bargaining power of suppliers will shoot through the roof. Two groups are important: the suppliers of capital and the suppliers of technology. Despite the emergence of new capital lenders, capital suppliers will gain some heft. Entry barriers to banking services will weaken, and thus capital suppliers will not be solely dependent on a few large financial institutions to 'buy' their capital.

Suppliers of technology services will profit even more. Currently, these suppliers have very little bargaining power, because banks today insource most of their IT systems. With the IT paradigm (see Chapter 6), and particularly the rise of cloud computing, technology providers have undergone a change of business model themselves. They are not selling, but renting servers and servicing them with software. This means scale advantages and a subsequent market concentration in which Amazon, Microsoft, IBM and Google have scooped 56 per cent of the global cloud-computing market. Amazon alone commands 31 per cent of the total – and the trend continues: yearly growth rates for the top four are between 53 per cent and 162 per cent (Synergy Research Group, 2016). Furthermore, since we expect more market entrants into banking with the blockchain, the technology providers' potential customer base will explode and make them yet more powerful. They have already made a crucial strategic decision that will enlarge the piece of the value chain they command by ensuring smaller banks use their services: blockchain-as-a-service (BaaS) offerings – a concept similar to software-as-a-service (SaaS) whereby banks have a ready-made ecosystem they can rent on a monthly basis (we will return to this in Chapter 4). Once on the cloud giants' systems, switching costs for financial service providers are high. This puts cloud giants in a very desirable spot with fintechs and small banks that need the necessary infrastructure but want to circumvent exorbitant capital expenditures. All these trends lead to markedly increased negotiation power for cloud-computing platforms. As a result, they can raise the prices and determine the terms of cooperation. This effect, however, will only slash attractiveness for those banks and corporates that cannot afford their own in-house infrastructure. Among banks, the rise of cloud giants will tilt the profitability ratio towards big banking.

The third force in Porter's model is the threat of substitute products. Currently, there are not many substitute products for payments besides cash (the likes of PayPal do not count as they build on the same infrastructure). Blockchain sets new rules, giving rise to true alternatives that can channel the money stream around the incumbent system. Hundreds of cryptocurrencies enable a P2P exchange without the need to have a bank account or to use a credit-card network. Substitute products are certain to put pressure on the margins.

Yet all of Porter's threats pale in comparison to the danger posed by new market entrants. The erosion of entry barriers threatens to smash the mono- and oligopolistic tendencies that exist today. There are no less than six major barriers as defined by Porter (1979) that hinder companies to enter the arena: cost disadvantages independent of size (eg learning curve), access to distribution channels, government policy, economies of scale, product differentiation and capital requirements. Some of these barriers will be unaffected by the blockchain, but others will start to evaporate.

The learning curve is one of the stable entry barriers. For example, compliance and risk evaluation require significant learning and expertise and there is no quick way to build up the competencies needed in these roles.

Closely related to compliance is government policy. It is still the major – though slowly crumbling – wall saving incumbents from the onslaught. The likes of PSD2 might level the playing field, but the institutional imperative of money will always privilege a tried-and-tested group, legitimized by a banking licence that confers obligations and privileges.

With distribution channels, the effect of the blockchain is mixed, depending on the target group. On the one hand, the largest channel for acquiring new customers is still bricks-and-mortar bank branches, but this is mainly true for older demographics. For younger generations, signing up for a loan or bank account by tapping onto an app is more intuitive than sitting down with a bank clerk and signing a heap of papers.

The entry barrier where incumbents really need to buckle up is economies of scale. Blockchain technology brings banking into the digital realm, and in the digital era economies of scale advantages diminish. Server resources can be rented and scaled at low cost, and the same applies to serviced blockchain software. It will no longer be necessary to employ an IT army to compete with the established players.

Minimization of risk also erodes entry barriers. Financial institutions are mitigators of risk, and therefore need extraordinary capital to provide for the worst-case scenario. The bottom line of risk calculations can make or break products, market entries and entire industries. This burden, however, is diminished by the blockchain. There are two main risks that might become obsolete with the new technology: settlement risk and counterparty risk (Tapscott and Tapscott, 2016). With settlement risk, the algorithm forces settlement of transactions so there is no risk of the other party not doing so. Transactions also become immediate; the time to settle the transaction does not take days or weeks. This means that the counterparty risk is also greatly reduced as it is very unlikely the transaction partner will default before the settlement.

Differentiation is another efficient entry barrier. Banking brands are well established, sometimes over generations, and although financial products do not tend to evoke emotion, the trust the brands signify is essential. Without it, no one would put their savings on the line.

The last entry barrier, capital requirements, sinks as well. Banks are still obliged to hold sufficient capital on their books, but most fintechs do not strive to become banks anyway. For non-banks, blockchain does slash the capital requirements, first and foremost with regards to initial IT investments.

The last competitive force that Porter describes in his model is called industry rivalry. Its intensity is a result of the previous four forces combined – bargaining power of buyers, bargaining power of suppliers, the threat of substitute products, as well as the six entry barriers. Despite the monopolistic competition, industry rivalry is rife in today's banking world, ticking most of Porter's boxes for this force. The competing actors are similar in power and size, the industry growth is sluggish, the differentiation and switching costs are low, and the exit barriers are among the highest of all industries. The blockchain will aggravate the situation further as the number of competitors will grow exponentially. The rivals will diversify, as will their business models, thus making incumbents' one-size-fits-all model fail for customer groups with non-mainstream needs. Switching costs for customers will go down even further. People might not even have to go to a bank branch, but just download an app and register.

None of the market forces will abate with the advent of blockchain technology, but nor will they be left untouched. Table 3.1 summarizes the overall effect.

Porter's model became so successful in the management world that many wanted to outsmart the strategy celebrity, to disprove some forces or add others. Most attempts to modify the model failed, however, and the five forces were confirmed time and time again. There was one suggested modification that did succeed: the power of complementors (Grove, 1996; Hill, 1997). This sixth power describes offerings that add value to other offerings, and it is only when combined that they realize their potential. Let's see how this works in banking. Historically, bank accounts, loans and debit cards have usually come from the same bank, but today this link is weakening and credit cards, for example, can be offered by

TABLE 3.1 Overview of the five market forces shift in blockchain-based banking

Market force	Pre-blockchain banking	Blockchain-based banking
Bargaining power of customers	Medium	High
Bargaining power of suppliers	Medium	Different per actor group
Threat of substitutes	Low	Medium
Threat of new entrants	Low	Medium
Industry rivalry	High	High

third-party providers. The blockchain, however, will allow for a resurgence in complementors' importance, thereby making retail banking as a market more attractive. New services will be able to be cross-sold – after all, the blockchain can breathe trust into so much more than monetary transactions. Once the traditional revenue stream loses significance, new business models will be able to come to the fore. So, at last, a positive message for the banks, although these are not windfall profits we are talking about. While there are plentiful opportunities to expand the core business, each requires a strategic commitment, a long-term approach, and an uphill battle against inertia.

Historically, bank accounts, loans and debit cards have come from the same bank, but this link is weakening.

The incumbents' predicament

In the early 1980s, if there was a synonym for the computer industry it was IBM. The US goliath was probably the best-known company across the entire economy, and at its pinnacle, IBM's revenues were rising more than those of all its competitors combined. The sky seemed the limit and the management was certain that mainframe computing had a bright future, attributing the previous slump in business to the oil-price shock of 1979. The recovery was just unfolding. Any CIO in doubt would go for IBM equipment and have the peace of mind that they would never be challenged for their decision. IBM's pampered employees did not even consider joining the competition. The only threat that IBM foresaw was Japanese competitors who could copy their technology and undercut their pricing by doing the same thing more efficiently. IBM responded to this by curbing marketing and sales. Customer expectations were subordinated to efficiency gains and another mass scale-up. The company tried to kill its rental model. Good financial results and an influx of cash led them to build lavish and expensive semiconductor plants. Tens of thousands of specialists were added to the payroll. In 1985, the company published unseen business results. Hubris wrapped its leadership. Yet only five years later, IBM's sales were US $68 billion, not $100 billion, its mega-capacities for production half-empty, and the customer base that had previously been tied by rented mainframes gone. Highly-educated – and expensive – employees hired only years earlier were either twiddling their thumbs or pocketed huge severance packages. The share price collapsed (Mills, 1996).

What had happened? The short explanation is that it was the technological switch from mainframe to networked microcomputers that almost led the company to fail. It is not that IBM's machinery was creaking. At its height, it was a well-oiled giant, whose brand dominated the industry. Its negotiation power with suppliers was beyond reach. Scale advantages on its production lines made it impossible for others to compete on pricing – and human talent, whether high-potential or senior professional, yearned to work for the Big Blue. It seems they had the necessary muscle to put every plan into practice. Could it be that IBM was so caught up in its power spheres that it felt beyond reach? Did the company not care enough about life-threatening innovation? This would be the explanation offered by the so-called 'Icarus paradox' (Miller, 1990), which describes a mechanism by which leading firms get so convinced about the superiority of their current path they do not realize how the ground is shifting beneath their feet.

Today, the finance industry is in a similar state, with a handful of big banks dominating each country's arena. Among non-banks the picture is no different. American Express, Diners Club/Discover, JCB, Mastercard, Visa and UnionPay make up almost 82 per cent of the entire global card volume – that is a whopping US $26,044 trillion.[1] All of these giants' balance sheets show them radiating fiscal health. So you could not really blame them if they were to get caught up in their position and ignore the potential threat of the blockchain; after all, today's model is not just working for them, but for all of their competitors. This is not what they are doing, however. Finance incumbents are among the first movers seeking to harness the new technology and protect their current businesses. Unfortunately, this will not leave them immune, as history has shown us. Take the examples of Nokia or Kodak, two giants that dominated telecommunications and photography, but saw their market share plummet with the introduction of revolutionary technologies. Kodak is a prime example demonstrating that incumbent's failure is not necessarily a result of its lack of innovativeness. Steven Sasson, a young Kodak engineer, presented the first prototype of digital photography to the management in 1973. Despite initial scepticism, Kodak still pursued the idea and in 1978 even patented the first digital camera (Estrin, 2015). Kodak had realized the new technology's potential and turned it into reality. Nokia and Blackberry were similar; these firms did try to launch smartphones, but they simply could not adjust. Yes, you heard right.

The most powerful firms of their age were incapable of jumping on a bandwagon they had already seen coming.

This inability to change direction has been studied extensively, and been given the label *inertia hypothesis* (eg Sull, 2003). This hypothesis tries to explain, scientifically, why insurgents can take advantage of future trends more easily than incumbents, despite the incumbents having all the resources of market-dominating players. It basically says that companies have a massive strategic commitment to the current way of doing business. The sales force is cast and trained to sell a particular type of product and service. IT systems are calibrated for specific business models and the mindset, culture and skills of the employees might not fit the newly demanded core competencies. Let's return to the example of digital photography. All of a sudden, the design and production of cameras did not require specialists to edit black film to perfection, but instead technicians to bloat the number of megapixels, manage digital memory storage and design intuitive menu screens. This change applied to the entire process, not just the hardware. Kodak had a virtual monopoly on cameras, films, cubes, paper and printing – most of which were rendered obsolete in the Digital Age. Similarly, IBM's physical assets were tied up in mainframes. Its people were skilled in building big machines and its strong corporate culture sustained itself by catapulting its most vociferous advocates to the top. They were all part of the long-lived success, had not seen different management styles and business models, and had never experienced technological shifts. This gave them tunnel vision and steeped them in hubris. Unlike incremental innovation that tweaks the existing technologies to make processes more efficient, radical and disruptive technologies alter the market conditions to such an extent that incumbent companies often fail to change their structure and their strategy accordingly. Firms that are overrun by disruptive technology have a corporate DNA that is from a different epoch. It is almost impossible to steer these supertankers into a radically different direction.

It has also been suggested by some researchers (Christensen and Bower, 1996) that current customers can be part of the inertia, because they reject the new products. When presented with the first prototype of the digital camera, one of the Kodak executives argued that 'no one was complaining about prints' (Estrin, 2015). Customer inertia does not mean a firm should dismiss customer-orientation. Rather, companies should also consider *potential* customers and anticipate the future needs of the existing ones, because soon they might be demanding different product attributes. Firms need to understand all the product selection criteria of their customers – now *and* in the years to come. Ask customers today what their major decision criteria are for picking a bank, and you will not find anyone shortlisting value-free money transfer services that work within seconds, because no one on the market currently offers this feature. Neither would people have listed the megapixels of the selfie-camera or the processor speed of a phone 10 years ago. The point is, customers only make demands that are within their sphere of knowledge, so companies have to anticipate what is coming in the future. If some banks start offering new features enabled by blockchain technology, then it will become a selection criterion and thus a source of competitive advantage. So tunnel vision is sometimes the problem for incumbents. Tesla was not invented by BMW, nor Airbnb by Hilton, and there are many more examples that support this point. In Chapter 4, I will examine how representative they really are.

Current customers can be part of the inertia, because they reject the new products.

To be fair, however, banking is not as at risk from disruption as technology firms such as Nokia or IBM, or even bricks-and-mortar retailers such as Barnes & Noble. Compliance, capital requirements and governance regulations are just some of the things that cannot be circumvented by technology. But if the banks think they can lean back on their banking licence, they are mistaken, as regulation is becoming more and more open towards non-licence holders. Payments and loans are fronts that are already under attack by fintechs, and if incumbents fail to come up with a practicable new technology, the first serious cracks will emerge in the regulatory firewall. This is a more likely scenario than it seems. Despite all the innovation power and dominant position that banking behemoths enjoy, their new products can fail catastrophically. The story of the ATM shows how an organizational set-up almost killed one of today's most widely used technologies in banking.

Ways to overcome inertia – the case of the ATM at Citicorp

Technologically, the 1960s resembled today's world in many ways. There was talk of radical inventions and buzz words that everyone knew would transform the economy, but no one knew exactly how. Whereas today the discussion surrounds blockchain or cryptocurrency, back then it was computers and online technology. Banks were in no doubt about the direction they should be going in, but the exact destination and path were a mystery. Citicorp tried to break through all this by asking the simple question: what do the customers need and how could technological advances satisfy those needs? The answer pointed towards online transaction processing networks as the future; an automated, connected network giving the banks' customers more autonomy and flexibility when managing and accessing their money (details in Glaser, 1988).

To transform this vision into a reality, Citicorp turned to the major technology companies at the time. Yet the tech leaders were reluctant to take the plunge and dedicate the huge resources it would take to develop such systems until other financial institutions committed to the idea of online transaction processing as well. For the bank, waiting would mean squandering the first-mover advantage, so they took matters into their own hands and tried to create a programming solution in-house. It failed catastrophically. Simply put, the effort fell prey to the problems described by the inertia thesis: back office was struggling to manage the increasing transaction volumes and even back then no manager would prioritize a development process over day-to-day business, as eventually they and their team would be judged by the latter. In addition, a Citicorp business manager at that time typically stayed in their job for two years. So why would they bother with a technology that might benefit the company in five years at the earliest? So, in 1969 Citicorp externalized the technical and marketing development and formed an independent company, Citicorp Systems, located close to Harvard University in Cambridge, Massachusetts. This location would ensure an influx of talent and was close to the computer-vendor community. After four years, though, there were still no viable results. As the subsidiary's name suggests, the new organization was not independent enough and it was too closely run by headquarters.

In 1972, Citigroup took yet another approach that was very unconventional for the time. They penned an agreement with Quotron Corporation, an IT firm from Los Angeles. The company gave Citicorp access to its processors, hardware and software patents, as well as 30 engineers tasked to apply Quotron's technology to financial services. A new entity was founded in Los Angeles, Transaction Technology Incorporated, and the 30 Quotron engineers were joined by the staff of Citicorp systems. Citicorp was the sole owner, yet the company managed to strike the right balance between corporate strategy and the necessary independence from the bank's operations.

The road to success is not easy, however, even if you have the right corporate structure in place. Citicorp knew it wanted to build an online transaction processing network, and it knew customers wanted easier access to their cash, without having to go to their home branch and speak to the teller. One approach was to install the simple terminals with cash depository and dispensing mechanism at retailer stores. But rows about how intensely the machines really stimulated retail traffic, and whether the bank or the retailer benefitted more, made it impossible to agree on a commercial model. Thus, similar technology was transferred to the lobbies of the 260 New York City branches of Citicorp in 1976. Retailers also agreed to install payment terminals to profit from cashless purchases. To use the ATMs and point-of-sale (POS) terminals customers received debit cards, or as they were known back then, 'magic middle cards'. Credit cards also had magnetic stripes that gave access to ATM services. Citicorp realized the vast application field of the new technology; customers could now deposit and withdraw cash or check on their accounts 24/7. 'The Citi Never Sleeps' became the catchphrase that signified this promise and positioned the bank for years to come. To ensure this promise was kept, Citicorp installed at least two ATMs per branch. It was a clear differentiator. No other bank could possibly come close to offering this level of service without investing years and millions into research and development, and it took the competition until the early 1980s to draw level with Citicorp.

So the ATM was a technology that promised to radically cut operational expenditure and enhance customer experience. Sound familiar? With the blockchain we see pretty much the same picture, so why are today's actors so hesitant? For starters, as was the case back then, benefits can only be defined retrospectively. When Citi introduced the machines, other banks remained sceptical. In the beginning, the limited transaction volumes made the costs per transaction so high it was cheaper to stick to tellers. But the breakthrough gave Citibank an unprecedented boost in market share; following the ATM

In the beginning, the limited transaction volumes made the ATM costs per transaction so high it was cheaper to stick to tellers.

introduction it skyrocketed from 4 per cent to 13.4 per cent. The new services attracted a new customer segment, which also made more efficient use of the underutilized branch system. In addition, there were more opportunities to cross-sell to existing customers because teller staff had time for more sales and servicing activities. In 1988 the customer base had tripled as compared to 1977.

How could a dominant player like Citicorp, who had everything at its disposal including a prototype and a forward-looking management, find the path to success so tricky? Remember Clay Christensen and his work around disruptive technologies? In it he did not only describe the phenomenon of incumbent failure, but pinpointed two major reasons for it. One is obviously the lack of resources. Competition might all of a sudden require different resources and make others obsolete. If you don't have them, too bad. This was not the case for Citigroup, nor will it be the case for banks in a blockchain world. Like the ATM, the blockchain requires specific programming knowledge, yet banks have already built up ways to ensure access to this IT know-how.

The second root of incumbent failure according to Christensen is the resource allocation process (Danneels, 2004); a firm might not be set up to enable the management to steer in a different direction. Its structure, its process, its people – everything is directed to compete in the old market. Even if there are initiatives within the companies, the new departments or task forces waste time and energy warring for resources – whether it is for talent, budget, IT or internal services. Luckily, research (Danneels, 2004) has detected an effective way to counter these problems, and it is much in line with the approach Citicorp took. To harness disruptive technology, it is best to set up a distinct organization. Of course each new legal entity also means an additional bureaucratic burden and risk, so not every innovation merits its own spinout organization. Iansiti, McFarlan and Westerman (2003) looked at when it would make sense to do this. They interviewed more than 100 firms between 1995 and 2003 and found that, if the complementarity of resources between the existing and the new venture are decisive and their coordination requires much effort, then it is advisable to keep a one-company structure. With the blockchain, it might make sense to separate the new venture initially, and then reintegrate the spinout company at a later date. The dependency on resources of the mother company is not essential and, in fact, IT legacy can be a major roadblock. Reintegration will be essential though; the blockchain is a technological enabler to deliver the services that banks are already offering today, and banks must strive to keep such spinouts close and aligned with their overall goals.

Fifty years ago, banks were privileged enough to be able to try things out, and to fail, without drastic consequences.

With hindsight, it is easy to pinpoint problems in how companies have set themselves up, but for Citicorp it was a painstaking experience, and the search for the right solution was far from certain. Eventually, the bank succeeded in developing an ATM. It established a subsidiary and staffed it with 30 technicians from a partnering IT company. They succeeded in the tricky balancing act of giving the new venture enough freedom and still keeping it aligned with the overall goals.

Banks must learn from Citicorp's struggle with the ATM, as they must from research studies. Fifty years ago, banks were privileged enough to be able to try things out, and to fail, without drastic consequences. Those days are gone. With so many challengers lusting to take over the payments and loans business, there is no room for error. The natural question to ask, then, is whether current market players are investing adequately in future technology.

Lip service or strategic priority – are banks doing enough?

Banks are certainly taking notice of the blockchain and 72 per cent of them have already embarked on their blockchain journey

(Deloitte and Efma, 2016). Over 100 have joined the R3 consortium while, in 2016, experts reckoned that the world's top 100 financial institutions would invest more than US $1 billion into the blockchain within the coming two years (Heires, 2016). But are these figures really that impressive? Compare the investments to banks' overall IT budgets and $1 billion looks puny. In 2014 European banks alone spent £40 billion on IT, and of this figure, a mere £7 billion (17.5 per cent) went into innovation, and the other £33 billion was used to patch existing systems (Skinner, 2016). At first glance, this seems a disproportionately small fraction of the IT budget to dedicate to a technology set to unhinge the current system.

In 2014 European banks alone spent £40 billion on IT; a mere £7 billion (17.5 per cent) went into innovation.

What about the other claim from the 2016 Deloitte survey – that seven out of ten banks are working on blockchain technology? This figure is actually somewhat misleading, and a closer look will tell you that 43 per cent of all respondents are only in the learning stage. Another 17 per cent are primarily active in consortia or other market intelligence activities while a mere 6 per cent are actually building a solution (Deloitte and Efma, 2016). This is a far cry from the enthusiasm promised by the initial figure. The reason for this sluggishness can be found in that very same survey: 53 per cent of bankers are convinced that consortium-driven, centralized blockchains will set the standard for mass adoption. The second-largest group (18 per cent) sees company-owned blockchains as the driver of the transformation. Very few respondents believe that each bank will need to create its own solution, but rather that a centralized or shared approach will prevail. If immediate competitors are perceived as collaborators rather than rivals, it hampers the overall urgency to come up with concrete prototypes and leaves them vulnerable to new market entrants.

So it is no wonder that bankers gather in consortia, but joining a consortium does not necessarily demonstrate commitment. The threshold is low; for the R3 consortium it stands at US $250,000 per year for a board seat and goes as low as $5,000 for a general membership (Irrera, 2017). Sceptics are quick to accuse banks of lacking appetite. Consortia are seen as a way of simply diversifying risk; if the blockchain revolution happens participants can say they have been part of it all along, without having put anything on the line.

In the past, banks have learnt that cooperation works, but tight budgets are equally to blame for a lack of maverick advances. Interest rates lower than a limbo-stick and increased operational expenditure forced by due diligence have curbed innovation budgets (Deutsche Bank, 2016). Bankers are busy increasing capital reserves, combatting a hostile regulatory environment, and pulling out of risky markets. Any manager wanting to safeguard their career will tread carefully before arguing for investments that will show up on the wrong side of next year's balance sheet. Amidst all the open questions, one thing is certain: the benefits of the blockchain will not accrue overnight.

It is hard enough to predict how disruptive the blockchain will be, but even harder to guess when it might happen. There are various estimates, the most reliable coming from Finextra and IBM (2016), who predict it will take the blockchain 5–10 years to go mainstream. It is not unusual for a technology to take years, sometimes decades to reach mass adoption, and it usually takes even longer for productivity to rise – as a critical mass is needed (Quinn and Baily 1994). This delayed effect does not only apply to IT, but other industries too: it took 30 years after the electric motor made its debut in factories before productivity rose with it. A new generation of managers were needed to fully grasp the potential and introduce new processes (Brynjolfsson and McAfee, 2014). This phenomenon has been dubbed the 'productivity paradox' (David, 1989). Whether we look at the PC, the dynamo or the steam engine, it has taken more than two decades and a transition from one 'techno-economic regime' to another to diffuse new technology. Each of those radical innovations triggered a wave of incremental technical improvements, which in the beginning hampered productivity. No one knows which applications the blockchain is still to trigger, but this does not mean companies can take their time in switching technologies. Research corroborates what you might intuitively guess (David, 1989): companies that switch first are the ones to profit most from the new technology. It might take years for investment in the blockchain to manifest in banks' financial performance but, eventually, it will.

So, we now know when to expect implementation and investment return, but we are still stuck with the initial question: are banks doing enough? To put banks' actions into perspective, more business theory is needed. Some strategists see innovation as something that, in a flash, hits companies and customers, shifts the competitive forces, and jumbles the market structure. The truth is, innovation does not come from nowhere. It is not bestowed upon companies like the fire of Prometheus. Instead, it passes three major stages: fluid, transitional and specific (cf innovation dynamics model in Utterback, 1994). Sometimes the phases might be shorter or longer, but they always occur, and always in the same sequence.

The fluid phase is characterized by high rates of product innovation in an industry, as firms compete in new product design development. There is no better example than the current craze for new crypto coins. Every day new ICOs are launched and new industries are supposedly transformed by some new token. Different technical and business models are invented, adapted or combined, but they are not improved. At this initial stage there is a low rate of process innovation. Companies are trying to get the direction right before getting bogged down in details. Blockchain is, no doubt, in the fluid stage. In the subsequent transitional phase, the picture changes. The rate of process innovation overtakes the slowing product innovation and accelerates the emergence of dominant designs. Products are fine-tuned, their costs reduced, and hard marketing wars blaze as fiercely as ever. Finally, the market enters the specific phase, which is when product and process innovation level off.

The innovation dynamics model is useful as it allows you to determine which actor will have an edge in which phase, because each step requires a specific range of capabilities. In the fluid phase a firm with strong competencies in the design and development of new product innovation is more competitive than firms lacking such strategic resources. Fintechs are more agile than banking giants. If you open the mergers and acquisitions pages of the newspaper, it should not be too difficult to discern just how in demand they are. They are the ones driving product innovation and the embryonic stage. Banks, on the other hand, have their hands full with figuring out which application group will eventually succeed and how to overcome inertia. Expect them to leverage their strengths only in the transitional stage. Once set on the right product design, their massive resources will trigger an avalanche of process innovation.

Fintechs are the ones driving product innovation and the embryonic stage.

This dynamic innovation model portrays the diffusion of the product in the market, and as such it is inextricably linked to the initial stages of the technology life cycle or TLC (Levitt, 1965) that describes the evolution of commercial gains. According to the TLC a new technology increases in market volume over time, thereby passing the stages of market development, growth, maturity and decline. In a diagram, the substitution of an incumbent technology by a new one ideally looks like an S-curve, since it has a slow start, a steep rise, a plateauing in the maturity phase, and a steady decline that coincides with the growth of a new successor technology. Furthermore, in the maturity stage Wolf's (1912) law of diminishing returns sets in, meaning that it makes less and less sense to invest in the established technology.

TLC's market development coincides with the fluid phase, as does growth with the transitional phase. Thus, if an innovator lacks the capacity to scale its technology it will end up with less money than an emulator who dominates the transitional phase. It therefore makes sense that blockchain start-ups are under more pressure to find a banking partner or to carve out a unique position than incumbents. This explains their frenzy and their all-or-nothing approach; if a start-up lingers in mediocracy after the fluid stage it will never make it big. It also answers our initial question: yes, banks are doing enough. They are doing enough because they do not need to churn out hundreds of designs, they just need to pick the winner, then improve and scale it quickly. Consortia, start-up funding and technology incubators are exactly the methods you would expect to see in the fluid stage. There are, however, companies that can combine the strengths of both groups: data-collecting giants. We will go on to consider these in Chapter 4.

Note

1 https://www.nilsonreport.com/publication_the_current_issue.php

CHAPTER FOUR

Data Behemoths are Coming

Myth: 'Fintechs are the banks' main challengers.'

Who are those fintechs that are making banks quake in their boots?

An old rule says the bigger the incumbents in an industry, the smaller the chances for newcomers. For centuries banking has been testament to this wisdom. However, over the last decade, the picture has been shifting. So-called fintechs – IT start-ups that try to improve or overhaul the current financial services value chain – long for a slice of the swollen profit pie. The most dangerous to banks are those working on blockchain technology, and at the time of writing there are about 1,032 in total (Statista, 2018).

Financial start-ups are securing investments at an unprecedented rate. KPMG (2017) estimates that investment in fintechs hit a record high in 2015: US $46.7 billion. The money pouring in around that time fed an army of unicorns (a unicorn is a start-up valued at $1 billion or above). By mid-2014, 17 fintechs had reached unicorn status; but just 12 months later the number had climbed to 83 (Skinner, 2016). With this investment came an overwhelming sense of optimism. However, after years of unabated hype, the money stream then started to show fintech fatigue. The financial resources that fintechs can tap have proved to be far from infinite; not only did the investment-level plateau, but it even experienced a sharp decline. In 2016 a meagre $24.7 billion was invested into fintechs, 47 per cent less than the previous year. This does not mean, however, that fintechs should be dismissed as a fad. They are a diverse crowd, and the negative 2016 trend does not hold true for blockchain start-ups. Chris Skinner (2016), a leading banking commentator, comes up with a useful categorization here. Broadly speaking there are three types of fintechs: the 'wrappers' that build solutions on top of the existing financial system and simply attempt to streamline user experience (eg PayPal); the 'replacers' that want to eliminate third parties and thus incumbents (eg P2P lenders such as ANT Financial or Lendo); and the 'reformers'. Reformers should give today's finance leaders the biggest headache as they are leveraging key technologies, in particular mobile and blockchain. I disagree with Skinner that mobile is so transformational, because wrappers use the technology as well, for example, PayPal works equally well on a phone as it does on a desktop. Fintechs tinkering with blockchain payments are the prototypical reformers as their aim is to circumvent or radically transform the current banking system. Unlike fintechs in general, the capital pumped into them is showing no signs of abating. On the contrary, it rose from US $441 million in 2015 to $543.6 million in 2016 (KPMG, 2017). These blockchain companies are not all the same however; some are coding new foundational protocols such as bitcoin or Ethereum, some are developing added-value services or applications that run those protocols such as Mastercoin, and some might be programming wallets, the special applications that help users to manage their crypto value. They differ in complexity, profit potential and their claim to power. Platforms top the list. Bitcoin or Ethereum are powerful blockchain protocols that underpin a host of other technologies, just like Android or iOS are systems on which millions of mobile phone applications run. Just like mobile phone apps, blockchain apps are striving towards omnipresence. Until recently, payments have been the core business, but loans are quickly gaining ground. In 2014 US banks earned $150 billion in the credit markets and Goldman Sachs (2015) estimates non-banks could snatch more than $11 billion of yearly profits over five years.

But what makes these start-ups so powerful? Why are they capable of grabbing such a large chunk of the market in an industry in which wrestling giants are locked in a dead heat? In management speak the answer is core competencies – unique resources or assets that other market actors cannot emulate. First and foremost, fintechs have the technological know-how that banks, processors and credit-card companies lack. Most blockchain start-ups have been created with the specific purpose of building blockchain platforms or applications. Founding teams consist of highly specialized developers; applications do not have to be tailored to existing legacy infrastructure; and the tentative culture needed to succeed in the embryonic stage of the technology life cycle permeates their offices and garages. If a new route appears, they can explore it instantly. If along the way it proves to be promising, they can join forces with other courageous travellers. If a project then reaches a dead end, it can be cut without heads rolling or a shareholder rebellion. The young and mostly small-sized fintechs have the agility and flexibility to be able to follow the direction of the market with ease. Nothing makes this clearer than the example of credit decisions. While banks might take weeks to decide, P2P lending occurs in seconds. Fintechs start with a clean slate and can devote their entire energy to new products. Banks, on the other hand, have to pump more than 70 per cent of their IT expenses into keeping legacy systems running, leaving a mere $50 billion for innovation.

Furthermore, a study by Citi GPS (2016) found that the ratio between maintenance and new development is worsening, which is a troubling trend for the banks.

Despite all these competitive advantages, there are areas where fintechs cannot currently compete with the banks. They lack their customer intimacy; they do not own complete credit histories or knowledge about savings and spending habits of millions of clients. They also lack a scalable technological infrastructure; the Visa network alone is more than 60 times bigger than all of the world's bitcoin activities (Coinometrics, 2016). Above all else, fintechs cannot compete with the two biggest areas that banks traditionally excel in – a strong brand and financial resources. Even with the aforementioned rise in investment, the money flowing into the whole fintech industry only totals about $0.5 billion, an amount that pales in comparison to the financial muscle of just a single bank. Ergo, it is hard to believe that fintechs could shoulder the entire payment segment any time soon, let alone the entire banking or finance industry.

Fintechs cannot compete with the two biggest areas banks traditionally excel in – a strong brand and financial resources.

Brushing all these concerns aside, commentators are quick to point to the colossal downfalls of Nokia or Kodak that we looked at in Chapter 3. Bitcoin is hyped by the pundits, who tend to play down its technical restrictions, claiming that, just like telephony and photography, bitcoin will turn banking upside down once the details are fixed. As we have seen in previous chapters, the frenzy is not confined to blogs or LinkedIn posts; serious journals have joined the debate with academics systematically documenting how creative destruction brings down industry leaders. The inertia thesis, for example, provided a scientific explanation of why incumbents fail despite their massive resources. Clay Christensen, father of the 'creative destruction' concept, is still one of the few names regularly highlighted from the Harvard Business School cadre (*The Economist,* 2017), despite his most well-known work dating from 1997. Blockchain enthusiasts quote these works to breathe authority into their bleak prognosis for banks and other incumbents.

However, a look at the numbers shows that giants crumbling because of inertia is very much the exception rather than the rule, and study after study refutes the claim that newcomers drive innovation. Chandy and Tellis (2000) examined radical product innovations over 150 years and found that, since the Second World War, three-quarters of game-changing innovation has come from incumbents. Others (Klepper and Simons, 2000) point out that all American TV producers came from a radio-manufacturing background. Methe *et al* (1997) studied telecommunications and medical device manufacturers, showing that incumbents introduced most major innovation. Listening to customers' needs before others has proven the best way to stay ahead of the pack over and over again, self-cannibalization or not. To be fair, even avid proponents of the creative destruction concept such as Christensen (Christensen and Bower, 1996) refute the claim that incumbent firms always fall prey to competence-destroying innovation. But the complexity of their work is not something that fits into a tweet or 200-word op-ed. It sometimes seems that popular debate does not only neglect the detail of these ground-breaking books and papers, but also the spirit in which they were written. From the pundits' vantage point it is understandable: the fall of Kodak sends larger shockwaves than a series of incremental improvements by a market leader. But how was this simplistic notion able to take hold? How could the buzz grow so loud?

The answer lies in the underlying archetypal story structure behind the scenario. It triggers one of our most powerful cultural frames: the David versus Goliath frame. The small, but righteous David faces an insurmountable challenge against the giant Goliath and triumphs against all odds. It is a story that works particularly well, because we all know its basic outline. Encoded in our cultural DNA, it is a storyline every child learns growing up, and it is repeated time and again – in the Bible, in cartoons, in movies. Research by communication scientists found that this frame automatically and subconsciously channels humans' perceptions and expectations (Dahinden, 2006). The normative implications for the banking world could not be clearer: big incumbents are squeezing people, and only an agile, underestimated hero can bring them down.

The financial crisis of 2008 gave rise to enormous anti-banking sentiment amongst the general public. Whatever newspaper you opened, whichever TV channel you watched, you could not escape the notion that it was bankers' greed that cost jobs and prosperity around the globe and displaced people from their homes. This pent-up anger persists today and can be reignited in everyday life when consumers see transaction charges for moving digital tokens of value from one account to another. Naturally, they do not have an understanding of the complex technological and administrative infrastructure behind it. People are not sensitized to paying for it either, since interchange fees and discount rates are carried by retailers, not by the consumer. Most people have never even heard terms such as processing or settlement, and they do not understand why it takes so long for money to be transferred from one account to another when e-mails are received instantaneously. Cue the small start-ups, parading the blockchain banner and promising immediate and free exchanges. They draw parallels to Google, Facebook or Uber. Their communication stresses Silicon Valley's ethos of bringing prosperity and connectedness to the world via new technologies and human ingenuity. Media and masses swoon. They cheer because the outcome of the battle seems familiar, and inevitable. We all know how the story ends: Goliath is brought to fall with

Over the next two years $1 billion will be invested in the blockchain by the world's leading 100 financial institutions.

a single, targeted shot. That shot could be the blockchain, a technology that would enable the world to move value around for free. This conception ignores two crucial points: first, fintechs are fuelled by incumbents' capital. Over the next two years $1 billion will be invested in the blockchain by the world's leading 100 financial institutions (Heires, 2016). Industry experts also reckon that banks' efforts at revolutionizing financial technology are at least as serious and promising as those of fintechs. This is particularly true in Europe, where today's finance leaders lead the banking revolution just as much as the challengers. The United States is bursting with leading fintechs working at rapid pace, yet the banks are not far behind. It is only in some countries such as Japan or Hong Kong that fintechs are the apodictic major driver of innovation (Citi GPS, 2016). The second flaw of applying the David versus Goliath frame to a blockchain-banking world is much more profound: Goliath is not fighting David, but another Goliath.

Data behemoths – the real challengers that have managed to slip from the radar

In business, most Goliaths get butchered by other Goliaths – an inconvenient truth often forgotten about in blockchain discussions. Management theory makes the distinction between de novo market entrants and diversifying market entrants. The former are complete newcomers, the classic Davids; fintechs, in the case of blockchain. Diversifying market entrants, on the other hand, are firms that have been successful in other arenas and strive to expand their reach. This group is often overlooked, yet in most technological shifts it is the diversifying entrants that scoop the market because they are experts in capabilities that suddenly become relevant to the new product or service generation. They also have massive resources at their disposal, unlike start-ups. When the camera-maker Polaroid failed it was not de novo entrants who took over, but companies such as Canon and Nikon that brought their experience with optoelectronics to the table. The power of diversifying entrants is not just proven by anecdotal evidence, but revenant members of the most elite management strategy circles such as Michael Porter (1979) see them as the biggest threat for incumbents. The tricky thing is to spot diversifying entrants early. To do this, you need to identify which competencies are likely to become central once the innovation hits the market.

A technology like blockchain that challenges one of the world's largest industries cannot just live off programmers and algorithms. Distributed ledgers and applications are only a part of the computing infrastructure enabling payments and transactions. Storage, archiving, communication and file serving – the blockchain cannot work without these, and all of them gobble immense hard-drive space. Blockchains also have an end of life. When they go out of business they will still need to be accessible, with each ledger archived. Contracts written on a former blockchain need to maintain their validity – they cannot lose it because of a technological update or because the platform provider on which the contract has been written goes bust. This is the moment for cloud-computing giants, most notably Amazon, Microsoft, IBM and Google.

These giants must not be underestimated, or labelled as mere providers of raw server resources. Realizing the enormous revenue potential of the blockchain, cloud-industry leaders have opted for a differentiation strategy; blockchain-as-a-service (BaaS). We touched on BaaS in Chapter 3. Instead of undercutting each other on price, these cloud providers are working on BaaS, which offers the server infrastructure and the necessary software environment for users to do away with the complexity of setting up and configuring their own blockchain ecosystem. This news is not great for incumbents as they lose one of their competitive edges in financial services, as smaller companies or banks can rent blockchain infrastructure without capital investments. No software developers, no complicated integration with the existing system, and no danger of blackouts causing downtimes. Not only do cloud giants grab market share for themselves, they level the playing field for smaller banks and companies. The competition intensifies and drives down profits across the value chain. The functionalities of BaaS are by no means inferior to in-house solutions. IBM has a Hyperledger-based blockchain system that includes smart contact capability, and Amazon and Microsoft are following suit. The latter is even a member of the R3 CEV consortium. Adaptability is no issue either, as the secure environment in the cloud allows users to develop their own solutions. Cloud providers will also have extreme heft because they are very concentrated – Amazon, Microsoft, IBM and Google hold 56 per cent of the global cloud-computing market (Synergy Research Group, 2016). Despite all this, pure cloud companies will never be able to cut into banks' core business as they are too distanced from the end customer. IBM does not arouse the same cult-like worshipping as Apple; the really dangerous diversifying entrants will come from somewhere else: globally dominating data-collecting companies – search platforms, social networks, e-commerce giants – are often neglected in the discussion about blockchain. This is not surprising as internet firms such as Apple or Facebook have not tried to compete in the blockchain banking world just yet. These data behemoths are pointedly silent about the new technological development, and publicly they do not seem to be making any efforts in this direction at all. But that will change. In 2017, Apple filed a blockchain patent to certify the verification of timestamps (De, 2017). It is no coincidence that in a survey by

The really dangerous diversifying entrants will come from somewhere else: search platforms, social networks, e-commerce giants.

the CGI Group (2017) banking customers ascribed the most disruptive impact on payments to Apple, Google and Amazon (each above 40 per cent). The only blockchain company making the list was Ripple (15 per cent), whose representativeness of blockchain start-ups is often disputed because of its strong ties to the banking world. All other blockchain companies totalled just 9 per cent.

Apple Pay, Android Pay, Samsung Pay and Microsoft Wallet are all hints that these data collectors are making moves towards the blockchain payments arena and positioning themselves where they are the strongest: at the front-end. Google is going one step further with Google Wallet Balance, a Gmail-functionality that allows you to attach money to an e-mail just like a document. Even large retailers are fighting for consumers' wallet interface; Walmart has launched its proprietary mobile payment system 'Walmart Pay' (Walmart, 2015). Amazon is another company living off data and contending for the front-end. Using Amazon's interface and the payment details stored there, consumers can make purchases in other web shops without having to create extra accounts or share their payment details. Yet Amazon, just like Google, is also prototypical of the cloud-giants group, making it one of the main contenders for the global payments market. Those hybrids combine unprecedented resources from both groups and are thus the two super-contenders. You don't believe me? Just take a look at East Asia and you will see how the rationale plays out. Baidu, China's Google, has offered its in-house-developed BaaS under the name 'Baidu Trust' since 2018 and is being used for things such as digital currencies, insurance, billing and credit management. Tencent, another Chinese internet giant, announced its own blockchain suite in 2017 (Sundarajan, 2018).

Amazon is one of the main contenders for the global payments market.

It has to be stressed that the payment interfaces of Western data behemoths are not necessarily blockchain based, yet they have positioned the big software companies as payment providers. With the advent of the blockchain, the potential is there for them to have a competitive financial services offering and quickly gain critical scale, while at the same time circumventing the current banking system. Data collectors are the prototypical digital mindset companies; they are the perpetrators of the new business models and have the necessary technological infrastructure to underpin such endeavours. Their technological know-how, on the other hand, is questionable. Naturally, the ranks of software companies are bursting with programmers and software engineers, and even cryptographic experts, and their foray into the payment arena will have helped to build up specific expertise internally. As there are virtually no blockchain projects known to the public, however, it does lead you to question how many good blockchain developers really code under their roofs.

Today, customer intimacy is probably the most sought-after new source of competitive advantage. The likes of Google know what we search, what we write in e-mails, with whom we interact, and which places we frequent. Social networks analyse who we know, how intensely we know them, and which posts are most likely to grab our attention. LinkedIn adds an immaculate record of our professional life and grows the data pile by another layer. Online dealers can calculate which products we are likely to buy and what we value in the payment process. Our click behaviour tells them how we read, which adverts we respond to and what influences our willingness to spend money. With mass penetration of biometrics on mobile phones, software companies can even link fingerprints, heart rates, or iris scans to the digital profile of a person. This is all just standard information gathered from applications that most people use on a daily basis; there is an app ready to capture data for almost any area of a human's life. Apple's App Store counted 2.2 million applications in March 2017 while Google Play reached a whopping 2.8 million (Statista, 2017). These companies know how to turn that data into dollars. Blockchain technology trims transaction costs to the bone, and financial services can be offered for free. This model plays into the hands of data behemoths, whose business models are already geared to making money from free services. Selling highly accurate personalized advertising is their daily bread. We will look at business models in more detail in Chapter 6.

Globally recognizable and trusted brands are another major asset of the tech titans. Google, Apple and Amazon have been at the pinnacle of global brand-valuation lists for years. The gap between these top three and all other brands is stunning. Their brands are worth, respectively, $109, $108 and $106 billion. AT&T comes in fourth with 'only' $87 billion. Facebook is on number nine, followed by Chinese ICBC, the only bank that makes the Top 10 (Brand Finance, 2017). Global banking groups are strong across the Top 100, but the data behemoths are much more concentrated and less regional.

Thanks to the vast resources that data behemoths have, there are two generic strategies at their disposal: they can either use their brands as the key to a differentiation strategy, or they play the role of cost leader. Experience with making money from free services, together with low overheads, is a proven recipe to capture market share quickly. Currently the two strategies are merged, though Apple is more geared towards paid services and it addresses a premium segment with its hardware. At the same time, Google and Apple are leveraging their brands and customer intimacy to lure away customers from banks. Yet, as we will now go on to see, the example of Apple Pay has shown us that their successful entrance to, let alone dominance of, the banking world should not be taken as read.

Payments as the first front line and why mobile wallets are a game changer

Mobile payments, digital wallets and Apple Pay – who would have thought the excitement of getting rid of a small piece of plastic could cause such a buzz? The talk about contactless smartphone payments reached fever pitch in 2016 with news stories claiming you would soon be able to put your bank into an app – lock, stock and barrel. The curiosity far transcended trade journals and payments conferences; in a study of 3.5 million social media conversations, Mastercard recorded that digital wallets were by far the most spoken about payment topic, capturing an eye-popping 75 per cent of payment-related conversations (PYMNTS, 2017). The fact that this topic is so accessible fuelled the hype. Almost every social media user owns a smartphone and the process could not be simpler to understand: you tap the phone on to the terminal, just as you do with your contactless card. Consumers were familiar with the mechanism and they were mainly interested in the user interface. Discussions about the way it worked or which method was most secure barely made the news.

So how successful were all of those mobile ventures? Let's return to Apple Pay. Back in 2014, the year the new product was supposed to take the market by storm, cooperating banks paid 15 basis points (ie 0.15 per cent) to Apple for every transaction, just to be on board. Even though it was Apple that scooped all the publicity and grabbed the front-end, these banks were lining up to partner with them. All major credit-card schemes and big banks such as Bank of America, Capital One Bank, Chase, Citigroup and Wells Fargo participated, but it was Apple that dominated the news (Nykiel, 2014). Retailers readily bore the costs of upgrading terminals, trying to piggyback on Apple's momentum and a gargantuan acceptance network was built in record time. Yet despite the frenzy, despite the company sitting on a Croesus-like mountain of cash, and despite its cult-like brand appeal, customer adoption failed (Webster, 2017). Apple has not published any official usage statistics yet, but surveys suggest that adoption was poor. In December 2017 only 3 per cent used Apple Pay for eligible transactions. The survey only took into account adults who own a smartphone and stores accepting Apple Pay, so if you set the figure against the entire population and all store visits, that 3 per cent becomes diminishingly small. So the company that was spearheading the entire US mobile payments movement did not live up to expectations. Samsung Pay and Android Pay were no different: they reached 1.4 per cent and 1.2 per cent in the same period. Interestingly, Walmart Pay topped Apple with 5.6 per cent (PYMNTS/INFOSCOUT, 2018a). There are, of course, mobile payment proponents who counter those figures by pointing to two-digit growth rates, but they would do well to remember the minuscule initial base. To grasp the proportions, take a look at China. Its population is roughly four times that of the United States, but its number of mobile payment transactions is fiftyfold (China Economic Net, 2017).

So, unlike its Chinese counterparts that are largely unknown to Westerners, Apple Pay, Android Pay, Samsung Pay and Microsoft Wallet have so far failed to draw level with credit cards. Alipay by Alibaba, the Chinese version of Amazon, commands a user base of 400 million users and, as such, is the world's largest mobile and online payments platform (Heggestuen, 2014). Asians are not emulating, they are *leading* the way. The popular Chinese messaging app WeChat is a pioneer in introducing P2P transactions; Facebook is trying to replicate *their* model, not the other way around. Something is obviously going wrong in the West.

So what is preventing it from taking off? It is unlikely to be concern about the security of mobile payments. In the United States, 30 per cent considered mobile wallets secure, 64 per cent said somewhat secure, and 6 per cent were not sure (ACI Worldwide and Aite Group, 2017). These figures show that there is some scepticism amongst the majority of the population (and this is on the rise), but with every third American considering mobile wallets absolutely secure the usage penetration is disappointing. The gap between the West and China can be better explained by taking a look at the alternatives to mobile payments. When asked in December 2017 why they did not download Apple Pay, 48.9 per cent of Apple users responded by saying that they were happy with their current payment system. Of those who had the wallet on their phone, but didn't use it, 17.7 per cent said that the main reason was that they simply forgot about it (PYMNTS/INFOSCOUT, 2018b). There is clearly no added benefit at the moment. China does not have the same credit-card culture and acceptance network as the United States or Europe, and online payments are not as commonplace as they are in the West. So maybe mobile payments only work if the alternatives are not as good. A card is generally more reliable; it cannot run out of battery, cannot crash, will not forsake you at contact-only terminals and does not require a mobile data connection. Most people also carry some cash in addition to their card; like every complex technology, terminals can break or the internet connection might be down. The idea that mobile payments would allow you to leave your physical wallet at home has been debunked as a pipe dream.

There are, of course, some digital natives who overlook these shortcomings and are still using their iPhones to make payments, but Apple should not take comfort in this; it does not suggest that the technology is simply taking longer than expected to take off. This argument just does not add up. Platform strategies and double-sided markets – ie generating one audience to sell its attention or data to another – are a risky endeavour, and can be fatal if the companies pursuing them fail to capture a critical mass. Apple Pay is the best example of such 'platform ignition failure'. It did extraordinarily well with business partners to build a network, but failed to excite the masses. This again has an adverse effect on the other side of the market. Today, instead of paying to be part of the service, banks could charge Apple for access to their cardholders (Webster, 2017). So either Apple's margins will shrink, or user fees will bulge. In any case, the path to long-term commercial viability is narrowing. Yet data behemoths continue to pump money into payment tools, and mobile payments in particular. Are they just waiting for competitors to keel over to then consolidate the market? It is unlikely. As we have seen, it was not a lack of scale, but a lack of user acceptance that made Apple Pay flounder. So why, then, are IT giants so relentlessly pushing the phone payments technology?

To understand this fascination with mobile payment, we need to take a step back and look at the long-term goals of the Googles and Apples. They have subdued, in record time, mega-industries such as retailing, telecommunications, media and computing. Add to this list music, publishing and artificial intelligence and the picture gets even more impressive. But finance is the sector to top them all. The Holy Grail. It makes the world go around, so it is a perfect challenge for Silicon Valley. But finance is an enormous sector, so where to start? Retail banking is the obvious choice; having brand appeal and reams of customer data in the bag, it is much easier to tackle than corporate or investment banking. But even retail banking is large. Very broadly speaking, it helps people to securely borrow, store and move value, and only one of those can be the entry point for data crunchers. So let's start with borrowing: what about loans? Innovation affects ancillary industries – institutions providing credit scores, checks or ratings – as much as banks. But whether a critical mass of loans can be backed without financial giants is doubtful, and IT companies have not attempted to do so as yet. Calculating cost of risk and dealing in capital markets to raise the enormous cash flow needed would be a whole different ball game.

Would providing safe value storage be a better entry point? Not really. Banks adhere to rigorous regulations and have licences that enable them to provide the safeguarded and continued storage of money. People would hesitate before depositing their earnings in an account that is not backed by banks and governments, and losing your life's savings would be just a hack or a bankruptcy away. In the course of my research for this book, I did the test myself. I opened up an account at a coin exchange, set up a wallet, deposited some euros in there, and swapped them to crypto coins. It was lunch money. Yet, as real funds turned into an alphanumeric sequence a cold wave coursed through my body. With customer hesitance as the major roadblock, is it any wonder that data behemoths don't want to store money and choose to focus on payments instead?

Moving value is nowhere near as lucrative as actually handling money and having it on your own books; however, as long as IT companies stay as mere facilitators and do not actually handle the money themselves, they do not need a banking licence. It is the same approach as Airbnb and Uber have taken with beds and ride hailing. Yet despite neither employing cab drivers nor owning real estate, Airbnb and Uber are fighting legal battles over their responsibilities. The good news for fintechs and IT giants is that, with payments, the modus operandi has been clear and accepted for the better part of the last century. Payment processors do not need to fret over draconian rules; those are reserved for bank licence holders.

An analysis by McKinsey (2017) revealed that the largest profit pools along the payments value chain are located at the end points, as this is where the end-customer interface is. Why? Because it requires an extreme investment in brands and customer intimacy. Trust does not come cheap – and, of course, customer interaction is riskiest. A concentrated group of B2B buyers might squeeze your margins, but is predictable; end customers and their dynamics are not. Data behemoths are right to occupy these end points. But why mobile wallets? Why not simply introduce payment features into the existing interfaces? Why isn't it enough to attach money to a Facebook conversation thread? Because to become really big – and of course this is what Silicon Valley wants – data collectors need to conquer the point of sale. Sending money via e-mail or social networks would be a nice feature, but it is niche. Compare how often you transfer money to friends or family members to how often you pay for your groceries by card. Mobile payment is the perfect instrument to leverage IT giants' unparalleled databases. The only reason why the frenzy over mobile wallets had not erupted earlier was because the terminal infrastructure was still contact-based. With the advent of contactless technology this infrastructure became irrelevant. You cannot squeeze a phone into a card terminal, but thanks to near-field communication (NFC) technology you don't have to. All it takes is a chip and an antenna – whether it is glued to a piece of plastic, shored in a phone, or incorporated into a sticker, as was done by Austrian Erste Bank.

And now comes the blockchain, the transaction engine that muscles into the payment business. Harnessing it, Apple and others would not need to build their wallets on banks' virtual credit cards, but they could provide the back-end themselves, thereby capturing more value and leapfrogging the banks altogether. Payments become contested.

To survive banks should avoid the music industry's mistakes... and their own

Let's switch perspective again. As the licence holders, the banks probably are not feeling all that under threat; the contested transfer of money is just a micro-part of the payment value chain. In the United States it accounts for $2.7 billion of revenue, whereas the entire value chain is worth $249 billion (McKinsey, 2017). Blockchain or not, the bulk of revenues will stay untouched. Credit-card companies and money transfer services will suffer under the new technology, but not banks. This kind of rationale is typical of many senior bankers that grew up in an era of monopolies and slow technological change.

The banking licence might have been an insurmountable entry barrier 20 years ago, but the world has evolved. Exhilarated by the Silicon Valley hubris, potential competitors, regardless of size, are not deterred by regulation. Uber has not waited for legal clarity but has moved forward and created realities, transforming the transportation landscape before lawmakers even had time to consider drafting a white paper. Today, cities could ban it, but who wants to aggravate the electorate now that it has got used to better service at lower fares? Just ask the city of London. Millions of customers and tens of thousands of employees were up in arms after the decision not to renew Uber's operating licence in London. This decision has now been overturned and Uber has been granted a short-term licence to operate, partly because of the enormous public backlash.

The banking licence is not the only roadblock; US companies are subject to regulatory crackdowns, particularly in Europe by the EU Commission and local governments. The big four – Google, Amazon, Facebook and Apple – make the best target for commissioners eager to sharpen their profile. Unlike European banks, they don't employ hundreds of thousands of people and often work with tax-optimized corporate structures. There is not exactly a warmer welcome for Chinese companies either, nor is the red carpet rolled out for foreign tech titans or banks in the Middle Kingdom. Even in a globalized age, local and regulatory advantages persist. Hence, having the rule of law on your side is considered to be the most powerful shield possible. In fact, many a manager sees this as an invitation to focus solely on one task: keeping the entry barrier intact. Just how fatal this conviction can be is shown by the example of Napster. Napster was an illegal file-sharing platform that clearly violated all sorts of copyright and tax laws. The legal situation could not have been more black and white, and it *did* break Napster's neck in 2001. Yet it was not the plaintiffs cheering the verdict. Napster's foray brought pricing down to an eye-watering level, so who was standing on the outskirts, smiling? The likes of Apple and

Spotify. After for-free file sharing shocked the music world, labels and artists were grateful even for the fraction of a cent that iTunes shared with them per downloaded or streamed song.

Napster's parallels to bitcoin are striking. Both are P2P, and both undercut incumbents' pricing. And don't forget the cryptocurrency's original ethos of circumventing governments and banks. Eventually Napster failed, but it gave rise to new, legitimate companies such as Spotify that thrived in the completely altered environment. Bitcoins might shelter shady business, but it does not mean that its underlying technology cannot be used in a kosher way. Yes, banks have a licence to operate, but that does not mean outsiders cannot obtain one as well and conquer wide stretches of the market once blockchain pioneers clear the way. Once again, East Asia indicates possible routes for challengers in Europe and the United States. Instead of partnering with banks, China's IT giants have already been very successful in launching their own digital banks, thus cutting out traditional institutions completely. Alibaba, China's Amazon, launched an online bank specializing in microloans called MyBank. Tencent, owner of the Chinese social network WeChat, is behind WeBank, which is yet another direct bank. The enormous advantage these companies have over the competition is their marketing reach. Loans can be promoted for free via WeChat, a social network used by 800 million Chinese (Yuanyuan, 2016).

So what might banks be able to learn from how the music industry dealt with digital challengers, and fend off the onslaught? First and foremost, the music industry is a good example of how *not* to react, namely by fighting contenders in court. I would also suggest that they should not try to fight them in the market, either, at least not solely on the pricing front. Battles are time consuming and expensive. You have to dig deep into your pockets. It is much better to join forces with challengers so that you can complement each other rather than directly compete. As discussed earlier, the technology life cycle initially favours small and agile companies that are strong in product development. These companies are able to snatch a large part of the market until the life cycle moves on to favour incumbents and their scale. Additionally, the effects of the 2008–9 financial crisis are still being felt, with the fear of failure paralysing banks and holding them back from investing in innovation; another reason why partnering with fintechs is the best viable path. Had Universal Music joined forces with Napster, it might still be at the top of its industry's valuation lists. The advantages of creating alliances are manifold. On both sides of the partnership it frees up resources to focus on their core competencies during the stages of the life cycle when they are needed most. Both groups have specific assets that are needed for the large-scale rollout of blockchain technology. Fintechs can bring the technology to the table, while the big banks can bring their trusted brands. Most customers want their banks to be the contractual partner – the front-end – so it is very difficult for young digital companies to reach scale, especially when large sums are at stake. In the B2B realm this need is even more pronounced. Customers are unwilling to accept the counter-party risk that comes with abandoning banks; they want an established banking institution to be on the other side of the transaction (Deutsche Bank, 2016).

China's IT-giants have already been very successful in launching their own digital banks.

Incumbents' cooperation with start-ups is nothing new. In the pharma industry, for example, strategic alliances of pharma giants with biotech start-ups are fairly routine (Rothaermel, 2001). Although banking has been more sceptical of this kind of cooperation in the past, things are changing. The Commonwealth Bank of Australia has formed an alliance with Ripple in order to enable permissioned, blockchain-based transactions between its subsidiaries. Countless institutions are choosing to base their solutions on Ripple as well. Others like Barclays or UBS have set up technology incubator programs to harvest the fruits of (blockchain) start-ups (Wild, Arnold and Stafford, 2015). Fintechs are on the lookout for strategic alliances too. Here is a fairly mind-boggling fact: more than three-quarters of all fintechs see partnering with established financial institutions as their ultimate business objective (Capgemini, LinkedIn and Efma, 2018).

The benefits of these alliances should not be seen as purely technological, as some can open up different customer segments. The lending-platform Funding Circle is doing exactly this with Santander and the Royal Bank of Scotland. Usually, banks would not agree to loan money to customers who they feel are too small or insecure. What they do now is to send them to Funding Circle, while at the same time they are invested in the fintech. That way, they can serve risky segments as well, while Funding Circle acts as a risk mitigation tool. And the customer's risk profile can change over time. With this set-up customers have not landed at a competitor bank and can even be cross- or upsold by the invested banks. Goldman Sachs and Société Générale employ a similar model with Aztec Money (Skinner, 2016).

Yet even if incumbents opt for the cooperation approach there are still lots of questions that will need answering. How do you choose which firm to partner with? Do you go for one that builds centralized or decentralized blockchains? How do you decide which one is the most trustworthy? The last thing a bank would want to do is put their reputation on the line by associating themselves with an unreliable start-up. From the fintech's point of view, choosing the wrong partner could mean inhibiting its growth and squandering momentum. There would also be the question of the form that the partnership would take. What would the ownership structure be? Would it be better to have a non-exclusive partnership with a large, highly valued company or an exclusive partnership with a company you help to build? Would it be better to co-brand the start-up or allow it to grow its own brand (Deutsche Bank, 2016)? Most of these questions

Exclusivity and interoperability are difficult to balance.

can be answered from the analysis so far in this book. There is no doubt that the centralized model will prevail in banking. Scalability, cost and control will tip the scales. Regarding the form the partnership should take, history paints a clear picture. Given the success of the largest payment networks – SWIFT, Visa, Mastercard – which are all cooperation offspring, it is highly likely that a joint solution will hold sway again; exclusivity and interoperability are difficult to balance. At the very least, the underlying platform must be the same so that APIs between the banks work. The solution might be Ripple, or it might be something that works in a similar way to Ripple, but a shared standard is, without a doubt, the way forward.

So, to master the blockchain, cooperation is needed – with fintechs, other banks and even the colossuses from Silicon Valley. Marketers have been quick to realize this, and have already entered partnerships – see Apple Pay. Yet the real blockchain revolution within banks will only spread to business models and strategy after reaching the back-end, which means that partnering on the operational side is no less important. As we have seen, cloud giants such as IBM and Amazon are offering BaaS, the computing infrastructure with the blockchain protocol. There are lessons that banks can learn from their own past with this. Banks are infamous for their in-sourcing urge; they must combat this and outsource everything outside their core competency if they are to succeed. Today, banks are overwhelmed by their legacy systems, maintained by bloated IT squads. It is no rarity that a bank has more software developers than IT giants. JP Morgan's programming army is more than 30,000 programmers strong and takes care of 7,200 applications in 32 data centres (Dimon, 2014). We have already seen that most of the IT budget goes on patching old systems. Legacy systems are also a killer for cooperation; in the above-cited survey, fintechs were queried about the major challenges in a partnership. Almost every third pointed to a lack of IT compatibility (Capgemini, LinkedIn and Efma, 2018).

Aside from insourcing, it is also critical for banks to act quickly. With increased competition, banks, especially small and medium-sized banks, simply do not have the time to build up the infrastructure themselves. They need to realize that there is no dishonour in buying in external knowledge. Even the technology giant Microsoft is not attempting to build its own blockchain solutions. Instead, it has struck a deal with specialist IOTA, a company working with an alternative distributed ledger supposed to fuel the internet of things. The stance towards outsourcing shows just how diametrically opposed the technology and banking industries are. The incontestable insourcing impulse of banking must be clamped down on hard.

There will no doubt be some concern amongst managers about fuelling the competition. No bank would do that, right? As it turns out, it would. China's search engine Baidu partnered with the traditional institution CITIC Bank to create BAIXIN Bank (Yuanyuan, 2016). But why should any sane incumbent outsource services to aspiring competitors to make them even more potent? And not just power them with money, but with data, the very fuel they run on. Quite simply because the alternatives are bleaker. Data collectors are here – and both sides lack better options. While big banks might have the heft to counter and to redline tech titans in the short term, for smaller banks it will be ever harder to survive. So to succeed, banks must strive to offer the best possible services. If this means partnering with the adversary to bring costs down and materialize an early mover advantage, so be it. It is a necessary evil. But the outsourcing must be embedded in a larger strategy that cannot be replicated by data collectors. For this, banks first need to understand what it is that only they can provide.

CHAPTER FIVE

Hunting for the New Competitive Advantage

Myth: 'In a digital world banks have no assets to compete with.'

The power of firm resources

The previous chapters have shown that, although additional profit can be made with new markets or services, and although blockchain could water down margins for core products, for banks there is no way around competing in the retail segment. That does not automatically have to spell doom. Porter's primacy of market structure is not the be all and end all, and how firms position themselves can turn an allegedly forlorn situation into an opportunity. There is empirical evidence that intra-industry differences top those between industries as regards profits (Rumelt, 1991). Hansen and Wernerfelt (1989) found that HR management and organizational climate accounted for more performance variance than market share or industry. Powell (1992a, 1992b) showed that industry effects and competitive positioning were not as influential as organizational factors. These and other findings contradict Porter's competitive-strategy school of thought. In addition, such empirical studies led to the prominence of another paradigm in strategic literature, namely the firm-level efficiency approaches. These have two major strands, namely the resource-based perspective (Penrose, 1959; Prahalad and Hamel, 1990; Goddard, 1997) and the dynamic capabilities perspective (Teece, Pisano and Shuen, 1997). Interested readers can dig into more detail starting with these works, but the point to stress here is that incumbents can improve their position by finding and honing the right core competencies instead of being wrapped in paralysis by dread from new technology and market conditions.

Unlike the Porter approach, the firm-level perspective does not advocate entering an arena where the five forces are weak, but suggests instead that companies should focus on their unique resources and use these to gain advantage. In a seminal article Prahalad and Hamel (1990) suggest that companies should limit themselves to their core competencies and outsource any tasks that are not directly at their core. Naturally, the fit of core competencies to market requirements should determine where the firm competes – this fit is essential. It would need to be revised constantly in order to master innovation – radical innovation in particular. What you need to understand is that when researchers talk about technological breakthroughs being disruptive they do not mean disruptive to products or industries, but disruptive to certain competencies. Take Mergenthaler Linotype, a typesetter manufacturer. You would expect this kind of company to have gone out of business with the transition from typewriter to computer

Banks have significant core competencies that will outlive the blockchain revolution.

keyboard, but Mergenthaler didn't. It led its industry for over a century, mastering three major technological shifts. Why was it so successful? One of their main assets was to own a proprietary font, and though the typesetter industry was brought down by innovation, font libraries were not. Mergenthaler understood which of its unique strengths would be required in the future (Tripsas, 1997). The point is, banks have significant core competencies that will outlive the blockchain revolution, and the relevance of some of their competencies may even increase.

No firm will find a perfect fit between its current capabilities and industry requirements. The good news is that competencies are not static. The bad news? Some companies find it easy to adapt, but others less so as they lack 'dynamic capabilities', that is, the ability to build up or redirect competencies (Teece, Pisano and Shuen, 1997). So change requires strategic far-sightedness at the top, but also elasticity throughout the entire organization.

Achieving the best possible fit starts by identifying which competencies will be needed, which competencies you possess, and how to close the gap. Ideally, the new competencies will be difficult to imitate, and therefore will need to be *built*. With enough investment you can cull technical knowledge rather quickly, but corporate culture, values and processes are way harder to acquire. Research has also confirmed that these competencies are more crucial. Mata, Fuerst and Barney (1995) found that it is neither capital, nor proprietary technology, nor technical skills that are the major source of sustained competitive advantage, but human resources.

Banks are global supertankers. Security and trust have been ingrained in their DNA for centuries, and, even in a world where a transaction technology claims immaculate security, this perception of banks is likely to endure. The old yearning to have financial assets securely locked away will be just as strong in the future as it has always been. At the same time, blockchain is taking banking onto IT turf, where digital business models require different strengths. The problem for banks is that innovation and customer-centricity are at the core of the digital paradigm and are the forte of tech companies. This complex picture illustrates the contradiction between the competency sets for security versus innovation that will level the playing field and allow challengers to pour in. An organization would need to be schizophrenic to be able to lead in both these dimensions. So in this regard, banks are doing a splendid job by partnering with fintechs. As we have seen, they are developing necessary competencies in external, separate, dynamic units, sometimes shut off in incubators. This is crucial given that the blockchain is still in its embryonic stage and can only be mastered via a trial-and-error approach. Yet even with excellent dynamic capabilities, the potential for change is limited. Migrating from one competency to another costs time and money. Each decision made causes a long impact-chain into the future, so each company's competitive strengths are path-dependent. Firms make decisions that are 'long-term, quasi-irreversible commitments to certain domains of competence' (Teece, Pisano and Shuen, 1997: 515). The choices they have made in the past define the options that are available to them in the present. This makes it all the more important to perform a proper analysis of banks' core competencies before marshalling the resources to steer the company on a particular course.

Banks' underestimated core competencies

If one thing about blockchain's impact on the market is certain, it is that the nature of the competitive advantage will get messier, quite simply because it can be realized on more dimensions than ever before. Old competencies will remain relevant, while new ones come to the fore. The term key competencies, or key resources, is often tossed around recklessly, but isn't what is 'key' subjective anyway? Luckily, research (Khiaonarong and Liebenau, 2009) has come up with a list of criteria to determine which resource can lead to a lasting performance advantage and thus deserve to be labelled as 'key'. To be crucial, a competency must:

- have value (ie increase efficiency/effectiveness and revenue or reduce costs);
- be scarce/rare (and something most competitors do not have);
- be hard to imitate (if competitors cannot copy them without significant resource investment);
- must not be replaceable (if a similar advantage cannot be achieved by using different resources).

Based on this definition, we can whittle down the list of all the things banks do well to five dimensions on which financial service providers can realize a competitive advantage in the current world as well as in the future. We can also determine five additional dimensions that will be decisive resources in the blockchain era. Table 5.1 shows the synthesis.

TABLE 5.1 Important new competencies in blockchain-based banking

<table>
<tr><th>Pre-blockchain banking</th><th>Blockchain-based banking</th></tr>
<tr><td colspan="2">Proximity to regulators (bank licence)</td></tr>
<tr><td colspan="2">Legacy customer base and brick-and-branch system</td></tr>
<tr><td colspan="2">Brand potency</td></tr>
<tr><td colspan="2">Operational excellence</td></tr>
<tr><td colspan="2">Financial resources</td></tr>
<tr><td></td><td>Data and data mindset</td></tr>
<tr><td></td><td>Experience with digital business models</td></tr>
<tr><td></td><td>Customer intimacy</td></tr>
<tr><td></td><td>Technological know-how</td></tr>
<tr><td></td><td>Technological infrastructure</td></tr>
</table>

A closer look reveals that with the exception of the technological know-how and infrastructure, it is very hard to outsource those competencies, making them also *core* competencies in the view of Prahalad and Hamel (1990). Furthermore, Table 5.1 illustrates that, despite the exuberant optimism of fintechs, competitive advantage can still be realized by the same resources as in pre-blockchain banking. Though they might be at loggerheads sometimes, there is no systematic incompatibility between the old and new world. Banking is changing, but we are far from a revolution that will dethrone the old rulers overnight. To see why, let us have a closer look at banks' assets.

The banking licence

The banking licence has been a common thread throughout this book. We have seen its power in protecting the savings field from outside competition, but we have also seen its costs, its restrictions and its bureaucratic burden. We know now that regulation is becoming laxer and that bank-licensed IT giants are a viable reality. There is no need to go into details again, but just suffice to say that the banking licence is a major line of defence. It is not an absolute safeguard, but it is a decisive advantage for incumbents. Obtaining it is tedious; you have to go through liquidity requirements, technological security, reporting, compliance – you name it, you have to do it. At the very least it is punishingly time-consuming; in the United States the charter process of the Federal Deposit Insurance Corporation (FDIC) usually takes three to four years to complete (King, 2014).

The case of TransferWise, the company enabling Facebook's payment function, shows just how powerful the institutional imperative of money is. In New Hampshire the company got cited because it tried to circumvent banks and therefore violated money transmitter regulations. Eventually, it had to cooperate with a licensed bank (Kahn, 2016).

But a banking licence is more than a piece of paper. Over the years it has drummed a particular type of thinking and a very unique skill set into bankers. Banks are risk managers that are specialized in risk and crisis assessment, have the necessary resources to back up the risk, and have processes and human resources in place that obey compliance directives – competencies that currently neither IT giants nor young fintechs can boast about.

Legacy customers and bricks-and-mortar bastions

Legacy customers have always been an extremely powerful and cost-effective acquisition channel for banks. There is little movement of customers from one bank to another, or even across generations. Parents bring their kids and hook their offspring into the bank without costing it a thing. But the notion of legacy customers here means more than just an existing and self-perpetuating client base. Legacy customers tend to be insusceptible to technological advancement and, in the future, are likely still to expect tellers and face-to-face consultations on their mortgages. Predictions show that by 2020 digital disruption will have seized 10 per cent of the total US consumer banking market (over $1,000 billion) and 17 per cent by 2023. This still leaves a whopping 83 per cent of the market not shifted to digital business models (Citi GPS, 2014). It is clear that you cannot build a long-term strategy on a diminishing customer segment, but you can leverage it. If nothing else, it will give banks unprecedented scale advantages for years to come.

Banks that have slashed their physical presence to a minimum and shifted their operations to online services have witnessed tremendous growth, while the rise of the internet has seen many bank branches share the fate of book stores. Yet online and direct banks are not necessarily an evolutionary step. We are more likely to see a large-scale divergence between two strategic groups: banks that are almost exclusively online, and banks that continue to serve the diminishing but still gargantuan segment yearning for some physical presence. With bricks-and-mortar branches the banks have a very safe customer base that cannot be reached by fintechs and data collectors. It is predicted that in 2022 more than half of UK customers will still visit bank branches four times a year or more (Peachey, 2017). Retail banks are taking care of small businesses too, which have a very distinct need for services that cannot be moved to the online world. An entrepreneur running a hot-dog stand regularly needs to empty his pockets over a counter. Small and medium-sized businesses are extremely sensitive to changes in the branch network; a study by the University of Maryland found that bank branch closures have a long-term negative impact on small-business lending, far worse than the impact on private individuals. The uptake of loans has been shown to decline by around 13 per cent within an eight-mile radius of where the branch used to be. The really shocking finding is this: even after a new bank filled the void, the lending volume stayed lower than before the closure of the preceding bank. This is ultimate proof of the benefits of regionally strong banks. Relationships do manifest in figures after all (Nguyen, 2014), and regulators will move heaven and earth to keep open the banks that pump capital to all corners of the country, especially the far-flung ones.

With bricks-and-mortar branches the banks have a very safe customer base that cannot be reached by fintechs and data collectors.

If branches are still important, then why are their numbers plunging? Perhaps they are not declining all that rapidly after all. Reports of the dying branch are hugely hyperbolic. In the United States the ratio of branches to inhabitants decreased by 9.8 per cent from 2009 to 2014 – obviously a difficult period of reconsolidation in the aftermath of the financial crisis. There has been some recovery since 2014, however, and a slight upward trend has been reported. In 2016 the branch density stood at 33 bank locations per 100,000 inhabitants compared to 32 in 2014 (World Bank, 2018).

So while it is true that digitalization is making its mark, a large part of the population is simply unreachable for digital banks or blockchain companies. Rather than being torn down, branches need to be reformed, opening hours adapted to the 21st century (how many working individuals have the time to visit a branch between 9 am and 5 pm?), and staff and tasks streamlined. I argue that branches should be seen as a sales channel rather than as expenditure necessary to provide services, a sales channel that is incontestable by the new financial players. However, in order for branches to prosper in this capacity they must be overhauled and the service levels drastically enhanced.

Brand potency

Big bank brands have always fostered trust, but people have not opened a bank account at Deutsche Bank or HSBC because they thought it is where their money would be safest; the banking licence has always meant that every certified bank has a deposit guarantee by the government. People chose a bank because it was the first to come to mind – 'top-of-mind awareness' in marketing speak. Brand presence in ads and branches mattered far more than what you associated with it. Messages all sounded alike; analysts would have had a hard time drawing any kind of matrix that didn't show the competition packed in the same quadrant. Brand power will come to mean so much more in a blockchain world. Being able to access non-government-backed financial services will mean that brand attributes, and not just brand presence, will become increasingly important. Furthermore, these attributes could be turned into a fully blown competitive advantage. It also means that fintechs and IT giants will vie for the attributes that banks have by default – reliability, continuity, security, trust. When quizzed about the rationale for partnering with established financial institutions, 66.4 per cent of fintechs said that brand power was decisive – the highest score of any response (Capgemini, LinkedIn and Efma, 2018).

Many a bank's brand is recognized globally, yet the importance of the brand also merits the question of how to enhance the brand image in future. Conversions for print, TV and direct mail are declining steadily. Traditional segmentation and marketing campaigns do not work the way they used to. Tech giants and social media platforms do not spend a dime on the traditional channels, yet they have unprecedented global brand awareness. They have also come a fair way on the trust axis; we are already entrusting them with our payment data, e-mails or geolocation. But trust means many things. It means believing the company will not go bankrupt in our lifetime, will not run away with our money, and will not send a scoundrel to break our thumbs if we don't pay our loan instalment. Data collectors might one day excel on all those dimensions. But trust also means that banks don't share our account data, patterns of our consumption behaviour, or the identities of people we do transactions with; this is a fundamental requirement for so many people. Awareness about data security is ballooning, yet privacy and data protection are the very antipode of data collectors' nature. The marketing miracle that will put customers' minds at rest about this has yet to be invented.

Operational excellence and financial resources

Like all incumbents, banks have, quite simply, become good at what they do; they have reached operational excellence. This might not be true in all areas – I know you're thinking about IT right now – but for the most part they are well-oiled machines. These machines are fuelled by huge war chests. The latest financial crisis has damaged banks' willingness to invest in innovation, but this does not mean that money cannot be mobilized if there is a real need. Banks currently hold $13.2 trillion in deposits in the United States alone (Trefis Team, 2017), and even potential competitors are coming to them cap in hand, asking for loans or investments. Having such enormous amounts of cash translates to being able to push the credit business to a scale that others cannot.

Customer intimacy

Customer intimacy is a major resource that, so far, has been largely untapped by the banks (Deutsche Bank, 2016). Customer intimacy is a broad concept and includes things we have already mentioned – distribution channels or brand strength – but also more soft competencies such as understanding the customers' needs, their buying journey and their communication needs (Danneels, 2004). As we will see later, knowing your customer is imperative in order to succeed with digital business models, yet banks' client bases have been mostly static. Banks can already map life events based on financial patterns, but they lack the experience to triangulate it with other data. They neither have access to the trove of databases nor to the myriad of data scientists that their Silicon Valley challengers do. Moreover, their data ownership of the financial history is being dismantled by regulators. PSD2 foresees that banks will have to share their APIs with third parties. Consumers can easily give companies consent to peek into their bank accounts and track the monetary movements therein.

Technological infrastructure

To run blockchains a large, sophisticated and redundant IT infrastructure is needed. Fintechs don't have it, but banks do. Their data warehouses and infrastructure are carrying millions of transactions and store trillions of dollars. They have the advantage of a tested, resilient and large-scale technological infrastructure. Whether it is owned by them directly, by a sub-company or an exclusive supplier makes no difference. Imitation is hard. Heavy infrastructure is a double-edged sword, though, and, as we have seen, legacy systems are having a negative effect on balance sheets and corporate agility. So banks must find a way to rid themselves of legacy systems by transferring transaction experts and data centres to support new systems.

Table 5.2 summarizes the advantages that different actor groups will be able to realize. Just a quick glance tells you three things: first, banks are still very well positioned to keep the edge. Second, data behemoths can realize advantages on many more dimensions than the much-hyped fintechs. Third, banks should be looking to enter alliances with fintechs as the two groups are perfectly complementary.

TABLE 5.2 Competency overview of the three major actor groups

Source of competitive advantage	Banks	Fintechs	Data behemoths
Proximity to regulators (bank licence)	x		
Legacy customer base and brick-and-branch system	x		
Brand potency	x		x
Operational excellence	x		
Financial resources	x		x
Data and data mindset		x	x
Experience with digital business models		x	x
Customer intimacy	x		x
Blockchain-specific technological know-how		x	
Technological infrastructure	x		x

So now we have looked at both schools of strategy (market versus capabilities) and dissected the likely market trends and promising core competencies. However, even the most painstaking analysis is worthless without accompanying strategic recommendations. So which strategies and business models fit best to which actor group?

Price wars and how banks should react to them

If there is any term tossed around as recklessly as *disruptive*, it is *strategy*; pricing scheme, business model and customer segmentation – it is all *strategy*. As defined in management speak, each company's choice boils down to three generic strategies: cost, focus and differentiation (Porter, 1980). In other words, people buy your products because: 1) they are cheaper; 2) there are no alternatives; or 3) they have something unique about them – be that better performance, a more trusted brand, or some other feature. Of course, the Porter logic suggests market externalities should dictate which direction companies choose to go in. Yet as we saw in Chapter 4, unique resources are equally important when picking the right path. So in blockchain-based banking, each actor group will attack with a different approach.

Fintechs going it alone will have to focus on particular buyer groups. In niches they can capitalize on their innovativeness and keep pricing levels high. This specialization can either be geared to a market segment – say micropayments for bloggers – or towards a small step in the value chain. The bigger the step in the value chain, the more likely it is that they will need to partner with someone. Ripple provides the underlying platform for blockchain transactions, a profound piece of the process, yet without partnering with banks the endeavour would be doomed to failure.

It lies in the very nature of the blockchain to lower costs, but positioning as cost leader for the mass-market requires more than a clever app. Here IT-giants have the best hand. Wherever digital challengers come, they bring digital business models with them. In market after market we have seen what this equates to: quickly building a critical-mass client base by undercutting prices. Whether it is Google Maps or Amazon's free shipping, most services for end customers are offered for free. Besides a push in costs, data behemoths will also seek to differentiate, but this approach is a far smaller threat to incumbents. With Apple Pay, the Colossus of Cupertino tried to bank on its iPhone's cult-like worship. But banking services are different to smartphones and computer hardware. They don't emotionalize, they don't lend themselves to technical features with a wow effect, and using an Apple interface does not suggest financial potency or belonging to a peer group the way owning an iPhone does. Even Apple has struggled with gadgets such as watches and TV sets. Bursting with whizzy features, Apple Watch was to be the logical extension of the smartphone but they did not take off in anywhere near the same way. This is not to play down the strength of Silicon Valley titans, but to show that, whilst differentiation can support cost leadership, it cannot be used to break down the banking wall.

It is the nature of the blockchain to lower costs, but positioning as cost-leader for the mass-market requires more than a clever app.

So should banks pull even? It is difficult. Banks' cost structure cannot parallel that of Amazon or Google as they need to factor in overhead costs such as compliance, legacy customers, and bricks-and-mortar branches. Banks have trimmed these costs quite significantly since the 2008 financial crisis, but simply wielding the knife more aggressively will not cut it once IT challengers enter the arena. On the contrary, these overhead expenses are setting banks apart from the competition and allowing them to charge a premium. Differentiation is the only salvation for banks staking a claim in the mass payment market. They need to create something unique in the industry, on several dimensions. Banks would be well advised to pursue differentiation for another reason: blockchain raises the bargaining power of customers and suppliers. When this happens, tried-and-tested management theory has shown that having a unique proposition is always the best response (Porter, 1980).

Setting out for new oceans – a dangerous endeavour

Porter's five-forces model (1979, 1980, 1985) that we know from Chapter 3 shows that the blockchain will make retail banking a less desirable industry. The question then becomes: what can be done to counter the threat of decreasing profits? The classic competitive-strategy answer is to use existing resources to deter new entrants. Set prices low or lobby governments to impose restrictions. But while picking up the fight – especially on one's own turf – intuitively seems the right thing to do, research shows that avoiding battle often is the smarter option. As every general will tell you, even the victor's army is worse off after a war than before it. Troops are diminished, finances used up, and weaponry damaged. Business works much the same way. In a study by Teece, Pisano and Shuen (1997) they found that, generally speaking, more economic value can be found pursuing new revenue possibilities than engaging in actions directly aimed at competitors. Every competitive pressure impacts profits. The idea of choosing an alternative route is backed up by the so-called 'blue ocean' theory (Kim and Mauborgne, 2005) that has inspired many executives to look beyond their core business and market. This theory considers each market to be an ocean. In blue oceans, the creatures have learned to cohabit with each other. Every inhabitant has its area, and although skirmishes ensue in overlapping territory, long-term survival is not a major worry. But in time, these calm waters can see an influx of other inhabitants that colour the ocean red. When this happens, it does not make sense to fight them. Rather, old settlers should set out for new, less populated waters, so-called blue oceans.

Blue ocean theory owes much to the famous works of Joseph Schumpeter (eg 1942), who popularized the idea of the creative destruction of markets. Schumpeter was convinced that every time a new innovation is introduced, it erodes or destroys the old economic structure and replaces it with a new one. He was also a believer in the first-mover advantage. But while Schumpeter sees innovation as a viable strategy to reach the competitive edge, blue ocean theory considers innovation to be possible without competitive battle, by enabling the company to tap new demand and thus disengage from competition. This is a fundamental shift, because for the first time in strategy research there is no primacy in targeting a competitive advantage. Both schools of thought, competitive strategy and blue ocean, discuss innovation, but whereas Porter sees it as a means to win the edge over competition, Kim and Mauborgne view it as an instrument to create new markets.

So which of the approaches is better, fight or flight? Before answering that question, some more theory is necessary. While the blue ocean approach sees a positive correlation of competitive intensity to profits, the competitive view sees a negative one. This can be explained by the stance they take on the availability of untapped markets. Competitive approaches see them as capped; blue ocean approaches do not. What this means is that neither of the two is right or wrong, but they depend on the specific conditions of the market. If there are similar industries or customer groups that can be addressed with existing core competencies, then blue oceans might be the solution. To a lesser degree, the choice of the approach also depends on short and long-term goals. Research data suggests that competitive strategy works better in the short term, while in the long term a blue ocean is preferred (Burke, van Steel and Thurik, 2009).

Where does this leave us with the blockchain? Are there new oceans to swim to, and if so, where are they? As shown earlier, the blockchain will trim the cost of storing and transferring money to almost nothing. First and foremost, this means new customer pools will be tapped, namely all those potential customers who are currently not deemed sufficiently profitable. There are, in total, 2 billion unbanked individuals who could be added at negligible additional cost. These 2 billion are concentrated in the developing world, which would give rise to a potentially huge regional expansion for Western banks. In the Middle East, for example, only 14 per cent of adults have a bank account and thus access to financial services. In Sub-Saharan Africa 66 per cent are unbanked (World Bank Group, 2015). At least 1 billion unbanked people are equipped with smartphones (Rangan and Lee, 2010), and if you own a smartphone you don't need a bank branch, an ATM or any other terminal for that matter. Suddenly the initial investment cost to address a Nigerian farmer does not look that frightening any more.

The second big blue ocean lies in a completely different industry. Banks could leverage the trust component of the blockchain to enter the authentication business. Everything could be recorded, from birth and death certificates, to marriage licences and educational degrees. The blockchain start-up Everledger is a case in point; this company has made a business out of verifying the identity of diamonds. Who else would be better suited to handle such sensitive things as official documents than banks? They have positioned themselves as trustworthy institutions for centuries and could leverage this to become digital record-keepers. Admittedly, this is quite a leap from where we are today, but it is possible. Banks have not only the right positioning, but also experience in complying with complex regulations and could be trusted with such a sensible task by governments.

Banks could leverage the trust component of the blockchain to enter the authentication business

There are plenty of potential new markets. In such a situation the explicit suggestion of blue ocean theory and the implicit message of Porter's five forces model is to exit unattractive markets. Yet will the drop in attractiveness really justify leaving the huge retail banking business? You might have guessed it; the answer is no. Citi GPS (2016) estimates that the biggest chunk – 46 per cent – of all global banking profit is made with personal and small to medium enterprise (SME) banking. It is hard to imagine how a technology, no matter how revolutionary, could cancel out these profits. Besides, banks' heft, scale, and their societal importance, are based on retail banking. But staying in retail banking is not just a matter of the big fat line at the bottom of the balance sheet, but also of achieving long-tem revenue with new services.

Today's customers of financial services are tomorrow's users of verifications or secured communication. If banks shift their focus away from their core business, they will most certainly lose out on the next big thing enabled by the blockchain: smart contracts. Furthermore, states would try to block exits, and those actors attempting to exit might fall into disfavour with regulators. Former customers would be allocated to competitors, resulting in scale advantages that might well transcend the retail segment. Research shows that divesting customers or customer groups can be particularly risky in industries with high fixed costs, because the company has to spread the fixed costs among the remaining customers (Vikas, Sarkees and Murshed, 2008). This makes firing customers tricky for banking, especially in a blockchain world where relative costs are even lower than now. Finally, banks would have to consider whether there would be anything prohibiting IT companies and start-ups from following them into the blue oceans. Retail banking is a fort not to be surrendered easily.

So exiting is not a viable option. The cut in profitability can be compensated by entering new arenas, but only if incumbents still fight on their turf. There is yet another way to improve profitability. 'Edge strategy' is a recent approach postulated by Lewis and McKone (2016), which has received a great deal of attention in both the media and academia. They suggest profiting from the 'edges' of a core business before turning everything upside down. There are three edges: products, customer journey, and the exploitation of underused parts of the enterprise. Often complementary products such as credit protection insurance can be cross-sold. Customers are less price sensitive to these than they are to the core products. Another example might be banks building their own blockchain infrastructure and then renting out excess capacity to smaller competitors. Edge strategy can be a powerful tool to boost profitability, but it only works if the core business is intact. This is exactly what the innovators are hunting: the banking core. They know the decisive battle will not be fought in some blue ocean or at the edges of red ones, but on the three main fronts: facilitating transactions, storing value and providing credit.

In this chapter we have seen that with the blockchain the nature of competitive advantage will evolve dramatically. The dimensions that companies have traditionally used to compete on are still relevant, but others have joined the list, making it abundantly clear that the Digital Age has arrived. Despite the proclaimed death of banks, they will still have assets to compete with tomorrow; they even have the potential to expand their business. But data behemoths will attack with a no-cost approach. So can banks' main differentiator be trust?

The decisive battle will be fought on three main fronts: facilitating transactions, storing value and providing credit.

CHAPTER SIX

Business-Model Evolution – The arrival of the IT paradigm

Myth: 'Trust can be the competitive advantage for banks in the new ecosystem.'

Why the security argument is a farce

For most of financial history, business models have been as stable as humans' need for money. Whether it was clay tokens in ancient Babylon or the IOUs in Renaissance Italy, priests and bankers pocketed a fee for running accounts, moving money or lending capital. Whether they pinched off interest or a fixed sum makes no difference. At a certain point fees on storing money were compensated by lending that money to someone else for higher interest but, overall, bankers never abandoned the fee-based model. And why should they? Its logic was straightforward: you paid for extra security. Stacking the bills under your pillow might have been cheaper, but the risk of losing it might stop you sleeping at night.

This logic is locked in bankers' minds up to this day – and it is not just tradition that confirms it, but psychology as well. After all, the human race is risk averse; psychological experiments continually confirm this. Among the best-known studies are those by Daniel Kahneman, who won the Nobel Prize for economics for proving human loss aversion. Imagine you meet a generous man in the street who dangles two five-dollar bills in front of you. He offers to give you one and walk away. Or, you can choose to toss a coin. Heads means you get both bills; tails you end up with nothing. What do you do? What do most people do? From a mathematical point of view the situation is obvious: there is no difference in probability to increase your wealth whatsoever as you have a 50:50 chance of winning $10 and the gains for the 'gamble option' are double that of the 'safe option'. So statistically we could expect an equal split of those who play it safe and take the five-dollar bill and those who gamble. Yet the vast majority gleefully grab the five-dollar bill and walk away (Tversky and Kahneman, 1981). Loss aversion leads to irrational choices. Just think of all the insurance policies people sign up to without batting an eyelid. It is logical to insure against an existential threat such as horrendous hospital bills or legal costs after a car crash, but some choose to pay a recurring premium just in case they lock themselves out and have to call a locksmith – paying every month of their life for something that will probably never happen, and if it does happen would only cause negligible damage. How often have you broken your glasses, your windscreen, or had a pest infection? People sign up to these type of insurance policies regularly. From a probability perspective insurance companies are like casinos – they never lose. Just like Kahneman's two bills, insuring against non-existential threats is proof that security is paramount for humans. People will make all kinds of irrational choices and pay through the nose for peace of mind.

This cognitive bias is exactly what financial actors are counting on. People trust established financial institutions and will flock to them, so why tinker with the prevailing fee-model? Come what may from blockchain companies or data collectors, challengers will only pick up daredevil fringe groups. This is not a water-tight argument. Just look at its major premise: do people really trust banks all that much? How about governments, the backers of the banking licence? In a recent study (ACI Worldwide and Aite Group, 2017) people were asked who was doing the best job of protecting their account and card details. In the UK, large financial institutions did indeed top the list with 48 per cent. Community banks got to 13 per cent, while 39 per cent of the respondents trusted large retail stores, restaurants or governmental bodies to protect their data. So finance incumbents do have a trust premium, yet 4 out of 10 people are automatically up for grabs if banks choose to run solely on the platform of trust and security. The overall trust distribution is similar across the world; yet in many cases big banks score even worse. For instance, only 19 per cent of Swedes believe that banks are best suited to protect their data.

Interestingly, governments (who should safeguard the functioning of the financial system) receive the most dismal results of all in terms of data protection: only 5 per cent of Brits said they do the best job in keeping data safe. This lack of trust tends to be fuelled by the susceptibility of public bodies to hacking attacks and governmental overreach. No story captures this better than the infamous 'bail-in' in Cyprus 2014, when the government unilaterally seized 4 billion euros from depositors in the Bank of Cyprus and Laiki. Every saver with more than 100,000 euros in their accounts saw almost half of their savings wiped out. Pension funds of state-run companies were hit hardest. The money was gone, evaporated. The parliament levered out. Confiscating the savings was declared as a restructuring of two banks rather than a new tax levy. Legislature and judiciary were bypassed (Traynor *et al*, 2013). Setting a precedent, the bail-in has shaken the belief in the rule of law like no other event in recent financial history. It is against this backdrop that interest in cryptocurrencies has been exploding and the bitcoin metaphor as 'digital gold' made its way into the public debate. All regulated financial institutions are inextricably tied to political decisions – another reason that fuelled the exodus of crypto fanatics to the alternative financial system. Imagine the consequences of a bail-in today: enhanced bitcoin alternatives abound and the general population is increasingly aware of the crypto realm. Governments and big banks must act cautiously.

Before getting enmeshed in a discussion about whether banks, governments, IT giants or start-ups are trusted most, a more fundamental question arises: is trust really a decisive factor when choosing financial products?

If bankers believe that, because people are risk-averse, they can lean back and charge a premium over challengers, they can think again. They need to consider convenience; time and time again we see how this factor tops security concerns. Just look at M-Pesa, an SMS-based money transfer service launched in Kenya by Vodafone and offered by Safaricom. It has taken the entire country by storm without even coming close to blockchain security standards. This phone application allows users to save their money, transfer cash to other end-customers, and withdraw money from so-called agents. Agents are comparable to tellers, it is just that they are people earning their living from something else, for example by running a kiosk or petrol station. In regions with low ATM and bank-branch density, they can earn additional revenue as human cash-dispensers. M-Pesa is basically covering the savings and payments functionalities of banks at very low costs and low security. It does not operate with a bank licence – savings are not guaranteed by the state. Nor is the transaction mechanism particularly safe – it works with very simple SMS technology. Now you could say M-Pesa's success can be explained by the lack of better alternatives; people living in rural African areas have no access to bank branches, ATMs or merchant terminals. This is true, but putting your savings in the hands of a telco without a licence, instead of hiding your savings in the house, is still a sign of risk affinity. M-Pesa is also flourishing in Kenyan cities, where there are alternatives. So could it be put down to cultural differences? Surely prioritizing convenience over security would not happen in Europe or America. Or would it? If you believe the surveys, indeed it shouldn't; 56 per cent of UK consumers say they would not consider using a store again after a fraud or data breach (ACI Worldwide and Aite Group, 2017). This is understandable, and you or I would probably feel the same. But are we protecting our data diligently enough ourselves? Are we ready to invest extra time and effort, let alone money, for it? The sad truth is that most people probably are not. Just look at e-mail encryption. Outstanding tools are available to protect the contents of your messages. Free software built on asymmetric cryptography can protect the most vulnerable contents of your private and business communications, yet no one uses it as you would need to download the software, secure your codes and explain the process to each of your recipients. The behavioural cost is just too overwhelming. People might think that they care about others' snooping in on their conversations but, when it comes to putting something in place that would prevent this from happening, they don't bother. This recklessness was revealed even more strikingly by an experiment in which random pedestrians were asked to reveal their passwords. Seven out of ten Londoners gave away log-in codes in exchange for a bar of chocolate. Every third person did so even without the sweet incentive (BBC, 2004). One might wonder whether these people would give away their door keys with the same degree of levity.

Seven out of ten Londoners gave away log-in codes in exchange for a bar of chocolate.

What banks need to learn from all this is that they cannot fight a cost battle, not against fintechs and data collectors that are slack-trimming machines. Differentiation is also tricky and it would need to occur with dimensions where customers are willing to pay a premium. Tried and tested security may appeal to many, but not to all. Even those valuing security first would need to feel comfortable about paying for it. The examples show that convenience and costs, not security, determine our choice of technology. M-Pesa will not be implemented in Europe, but blockchain-driven copycats are already under way: the start-up Abra can turn each of its users into tellers, while in the background the blockchain guarantees security levels unreachable by SMS or most other information-exchange technologies. For those customers who are adamant that a banking licence is absolutely necessary, there are direct banks that make a point in being blockchain led, but operate with a banking licence. Revolut Bank, which started in the UK and rapidly expanded to a host of countries, offers the basic functionalities of a bank – account, loan, credit card and insurance – but also lets you trade bitcoin, Litecoin and Ethereum. Costs are low, functionality simple, and cryptocurrencies accessible. It has also applied for a bank licence so it will be able to offer the same deposit protection as incumbents.

In many ways, the IT paradigm has bred highly price-sensitive customers who take free digital services for granted. In the case of banking, it is turning into downright demand. Functionality and ease of use become the main decision criteria. These changes impact products and services, but above all, they will have consequences for business models.

Market rules of the IT paradigm

The digital paradigm permeates all spheres of business activity – whether it is the openness of the geek entourage that makes buttoned-up executives of the old guard quake in their boots, or the technological trends that favour digital over physical services and exponential over linear mechanisms. But most importantly for the boards of incumbents and new entrants, technological leaps coincide with the evolution of business models. After all, consumers don't just change their attitude on product features, but also on costs and pricing. While 10 years ago no one grumbled about paying for a wire transfer, in today's hyper-connected world people have a different perception of what the update of two ledgers should cost. It would be dangerous to allow current business models to cloud future strategy. Look at Polaroid. When the management decided that consumables (ie films) were the place to make money and the hardware (ie the camera) was just an enabler, it did not see the changing tides of time. Digitalization swapped the profit generator, felling the film – the blade in management speak – and camera makers were forced to charge for the hardware. Eventually, the digitalization of the industry caught Polaroid napping (Danneels, 2004).

Each era carries with it a preferred business model. Broadly speaking there are four major ways of earning money. Each of them is enabled by different technologies and assets, and each of them leads to different profitability levels. First, there are asset builders that create and deliver value via utilizing physical assets. Steel manufacturers need large-scale plants with expensive machines. Second, there are service providers that base their value delivery on their human capital. A cleaning company might not require machinery, but squads of personnel. Third, technology creators use intellectual capital to sell their ideas and intellectual property such as software. Licensing costs you pay for your computer's Windows system go to highly-trained software developers who build the system and keep it running. Finally, network orchestrators employ their network capital to deliver value, ie giving the customers access to other participants of a network. Newspapers sell their readers to advertisers. Empirical results show that network orchestrators dramatically outperform the rest, but despite this there are hardly any companies switching their business model. The investment into the respective assets is too large and often companies simply lack the expertise to apply transformational technologies. That is why network orchestrators still only account for 2 per cent of all publicly traded companies (Libert, Beck and Wind, 2016a).

So what do network orchestrators look like? Orchestrator advantages manifest best by utilizing both technology and network assets. So unless you consider the printing press a late technological breakthrough, the aforementioned newspaper example is actually not prototypical. Search engines are a better example. Lowered costs and increasing speed are the game changers of the digital paradigm, and these two advantages are exactly the blockchain's value proposition. To capture the value of this promise, IT giants and fintech start-ups are providing analogously thinking industries with new ways to compete. Big data, two-sided markets and free-of-charge business models are just some of the concepts needed to achieve competitive parity with IT firms. For cameras, the evolution was straightforward. You could not charge customers running costs for consumables any more, so you had to offer pricey cameras bursting with features and megapixels. To keep customers coming back, the features were bloated exponentially and in ever shorter intervals. Cunning producers also profited from the edges – high-margin by-products such as tripods and casings were cross-sold. For other industries, the business-model disruption is trickier, but no less lucrative. Two-sided platforms work particularly well where people are least inclined to pay for services, say online media or smartphone applications. With this approach companies have to serve two customer sides of the same coin in parallel. Those two groups have conflicting interests and one group's size has a direct impact on the other's (Rochet and Tirole, 2006). If I bombard app users with banners and pop-ups, I will scare them. If I scare them, advertisers will jump ship too. If I restrict advertising too much, though, I will not have the financial resources to make the product attractive enough to gather larger audiences. It is a balancing act that only the best can manage.

Lowered costs and increasing speed are the game changers of the digital paradigm.

Google's offering of AdWords together with its search engine is symptomatic for this business-model shift. It was the first scalable and dynamic two-sided platform (Baden-Fuller and Haefliger, 2013). The challenge was to create a great tool (Google search bar) at an unbeatable price (for free) to end users. In order to cover the costs and earn money, those end-users' attention was then sold to the second customer group in this model, namely companies wishing to advertise to individually segmented target groups. In two-sided models the fundamental question is always which side to charge and which to attract by burning money. The good news for banks is this: customer intimacy is the prerequisite for succeeding with this model. Banks have plenty of it, and they are not using it to its full potential today.

In another paper, the same researchers who came up with the categorization (Libert, Beck and Wind, 2016b) argue that, in banking, the blockchain will be the technology to push the industry towards the network-orchestrator business model. It will make network capital much more valuable than it is today. Banking is already witnessing the first waves of the digital revolution; digital banks and the closure of bricks-and-mortar branches are testament to this, but the major catalyst will be blockchain technology.

In banking, the blockchain will be the technology to push the industry towards the network orchestrator business model.

So let us apply this framework to the three major actor groups in a blockchain-based banking world. Traditionally speaking, banks can be seen as service providers, fintechs as technology creators, and the data collectors as network orchestrators. The data collectors therefore have the largest profit-reaping potential. It also means banks should not even entertain the thought of surrendering the front end to attackers such as Apple Pay, who demand not only a percentage of the transaction, but also dedicated and punishingly high marketing budgets. Not to mention the fact that it forbids banks' own wallets from being offered in its app store. Instead of giving in, banks need to orchestrate networks themselves.

It is hard to argue that banks are still classic service providers. More and more tasks are done by the customers themselves, and what banks are mainly responsible for are the technical assets. Customers are mainly concerned about the reliable functioning of ATMs and apps. The evolution from service providers to technology facilitators is in full swing, and, as we will see in this chapter, some banks are even going in the network-orchestrator direction. Sometimes it is hard to discern which of the four models holds sway. From flat rates, aggregator services, all the way to fully fledged platform models, banks are starting to embrace new ways of making money.

From fees to flat rates

A straightforward way to keep customers paying after an innovation smashes pricing is to introduce a flat rate scheme in which all financial services are included in one monthly or yearly fee. Telephony and internet services have worked with flat rates for a long time, and the success of Netflix has shown that it works for entertainment too. Banks are already familiar with the model: having an account often includes free-of-charge account management, ATM withdrawals and transactions – but in most cases only within one country or the euro area. In the blockchain age this will be insufficient as there is no justification to charge more for international transfers.

The flat rate model stands and falls with the services included in the package. Insurances, credit cards and loans – banks will have to decide which to include and thus forego the opportunity to cross-sell. The pricing is secondary to deciding what should be incorporated, because the crucial thing is that the offering covers more than just the basic services. Blockchain fintechs will most probably compete with stripped-down functionalities for free, in the same way that digital banks are doing today. We have seen that trust does not justify a premium, so differentiation will have to come from banks including more features in the flat rate package than their new competitors.

This route is profitable, but is it also sustainable? The blockchain will enable new services and improve existing ones. Initially, this justifies prices bearing a healthy premium in case the offerings improve. But the willingness to pay for differentiation declines as the industry matures (Porter, 1979). Thus, flat rates will only postpone the pressure on margins triggered by the blockchain. Also, as the life cycle of blockchain-based banking progresses and competition intensifies, banks will run out of features that justify charging a flat rate when compared to free offerings from fintechs. More innovative models are needed.

Banks as assemblers of financial tools

I have already hinted at the profit pools associated with accounts and money transfers. Cross-selling is the magic word. To do so, you have to occupy a certain spot, and this is why it is so dangerous that services like Apple Pay try to push banks to the back-end. If the triumph of the network orchestrators teaches us anything, it is that for profits' sake banks need to stay close to the end customer, not move away from them on the value chain. As we have seen, their strong branding means that they already have the prerequisite to be successful there, so the next thing for them to do is ramp up their offering. A collection of all banking services in one place would be a major differentiator for customers from a convenience point of view. For customers, downloading dozens of apps onto their phone or trying to remember multiple codes and addresses (a particular annoyance with bitcoin) comes with a significant behavioural cost. Having everything in one place, for example, in one banking app, would solve this problem. Like the fee approach, aggregation falls under differentiation, not cost leadership.

There is one more thing that all customers appreciate, regardless of how digitally inclined they are: omni-channel offerings. Web platforms, mobile applications, branches and call centres – users want it all. I might do 99 per cent of my transactions online, but knowing that I can go to a counter any time to speak to an employee gives a sense of security. By the same token, mobile-only banks lose many customers by not even offering a desktop application. Omni-channel servicing will prove a litmus test for data behemoths as much as for fintechs. Only those serving all channels can claim to be the best finance aggregator. Some products simply favour particular ways of interaction – a mortgage is difficult to explain and sell via an app, and IT giants often have inherent limitations – for example, Apple will not offer Android Pay. Banks, on the other hand, are predestined to aggregate various services under their umbrella and become the one-stop-shop of finance, not least because of their history of co-opetition.

Omni-channel servicing will prove a litmus test for data behemoths as much as for fintechs.

To build powerful platforms, banks must not attempt to churn out a plethora of apps themselves. After all, this would shift the battle on to the turf of their new competitors. Instead, incumbents must take advantage of the exploding number of fintechs and their focused services. If a bank lacks the knowledge about cryptocurrency exchange, then they should contract or buy an expert fintech and include their trading functionality into the app.

In this aggregator scenario banks move to the front-end as the single point of contact, integrating various blockchain-based fintech services. Value is captured by selling core services and by taking a slice from external offerings integrated into the platform. Theoretically, this can work one of two ways. First is the marketplace approach – banks are platforms that link users to new products by other companies, thereby collecting a fee from the vendors. Vendors still offer their apps and services under their own brands. As prototypical as this may be of the orchestrator model, it does not fit banks' unique selling proposition (USP). Google or Amazon could do the same thing. Apple's app store can offer all of those apps, and more, and probably do it better. Banks need to provide an added value besides simply linking audiences and fintechs, for example by deploying their omni-channel capabilities or bank licence.

The second option is more promising: banks pick the best start-ups and integrate them in a white-label fashion under their own branding. This still monetizes network capital but, unlike TripAdvisor or Booking.com that simply collect and rate what they can find via algorithms, the services are offered under the banks' brands. Indeed, this is also the modus operandi preferred by fintechs: 66.4 per cent – by far the highest score – favour white labelling (Capgemini, LinkedIn and Efma, 2018). The reason is clear: it allows fintechs to leverage banks' scale and to do so in many ways. If they provide the engine in the back it stays under-cover. Hence, they can sell the same solution to different banks. If banks insist that they don't do this, then at least they might be in line for an exclusivity premium. For banks, white labelling means that a far larger part of the profit pie can be seized than if they were simply the broker. It is also a loyalty transfer as it is easier to sell something under a big bank's label than an unknown fintech's. At the same time, however, it comes with technical, structural, legal and marketing challenges. Depending on the form of cooperation, the front-end provider is responsible for regulatory compliance of the value chain. Compare it to car manufacturers. They are mostly assemblers of components, but if the latest model's brakes fail, it is *their* lawyers rushing to the courtrooms. Yet banks have this exact expertise rooted in their core competencies, and it cannot be easily mimicked by data collectors.

The business model 'free'

Differentiation strategy or not, the network orchestrator model always lets prices plunge, in most cases right down to zero. As companies can earn money aside from directly charging their customers, they engage in price wars. Is it any wonder, then, that people are used to getting digital services for free?

The business model 'free' is also a result of the 'winner-takes-all' mechanism prominent in the digital realm. The assumption is that once the market is scooped, prices can be set almost at will and profitability shoots up. Thus, in a first-step, differentiation and cost-leadership strategies are merged, which quashes margins. The examples of lacking profitability are aplenty. For fintechs this market approach is tried and tested and many investors readily accept an indefinite postponement of the break-even point. Good luck convincing banks' shareholders of that. Investors in big institutions are a mixed lot. Short- and medium-term investors do not want to hear that for the coming years they have to cut back on their dividends because of a switch to a new business model. Luckily, there are ways to earn money while merging cost leadership and differentiation.

Transcending the financial

For many bankers, the blockchain evokes more fear than enthusiasm, as they see it first and foremost as an assault on their dominance of an industry. What they should understand, though, is that attack is the best defence. Yes, we have seen how payments can be a Trojan Horse out of whose belly tech-titans and start-ups crawl to conquer finance. Yet it works the other way around too. Payments is an interface to every pore of the economy. Leveraging a killer app can unleash revenues from corners never even thought of. Skinner (2016) illustrates this with the example of Shinhan Bank in South Korea, which has created its own restaurant app with payment functionality. The app spread rapidly through the market, so much so that other banks are now paying Shinhan to be in their wallet. It has captured the front-end and now sells its customers' attention to competitors. This typical double-sided market sends them up a positive spiral: with the revenue coming from companies seeking to be in its app, the prices or functionalities for users can be streamlined.

In Europe the same thing is happening. Austrian Erste Bank launched 'George', a web and mobile application for its customers. After the app rapidly proved itself to be popular amongst users and came to enjoy respectable name recognition, Erste's management started thinking loudly about licensing it to other banks, which would make the app a potential new source of income (Wiens, 2018). It did not divulge any details of the model – especially on branding – but it points to a new income pillar. Through the gateway of payments and financial management, banks can sell software products, not just traditional banking services.

It doesn't always have to be the software model. Cross-selling of non-IT-related by-products can be equally profitable. Ukrainian Privatbank banked on people's mistrust towards e-commerce by making use of an asset that is constantly under assault: the branch system. People could shop online using the branch's tablets and let the goods be delivered directly to the bank (PrivatBank, 2016). The app approach will definitely be the more well-trodden path, but this unusual innovation from Privatbank shows the potential for out-of-the-box revenue streams, as well as showing that some business models depend on the local context. In the United States, where online shopping is an everyday experience for most people, it is hard to imagine this service working. It is in local refinements like these that data behemoths' one-size-fits-all approach can be countered.

Freemium – why free must not be free

The term 'freemium' also denotes a model in which the basic services are available at no charge, but then revenue is made by offering a premium version. For example, transactions of up to US $100, or five transactions per month, could be free, while any transactions exceeding these limits could be charged either per service or per fixed subscription rate. This has the advantage of rapidly increasing the number of customers, yet the conversion rate from non-paying to paying customers is critical. This model is also better suited to data collectors and fintechs, as they have been working with it since their inception. The other route is to seek out the premium users from the start with a weak basic and strong premium offering. This is where the differentiation part comes in: if banks manage to assemble more and better tools, the majority of premium users will accept higher rates.

Monetizing data

When giving away blockchain-based financial services for free, money can also be made by selling the generated reams of data – either as raw data or in the form of highly targeted audiences. As the actor group's name suggests, this business model is the realm of data collectors. They can combine the insights with the profiles already being built by data from search engines, social networks, phones or smart-watch usage. For Google or Apple, the way the customer pays is just another part of the jigsaw puzzle they can use to enhance their target-group accuracy when selling to advertisers and coming up with new products. It may also be used by fintech companies, but small specialized ones lack the scale to integrate financial data with the rest of the digital footprint. It would be somewhat less sophisticated, but they could place targeted advertisements in their applications, or they could sell the raw data to other companies where legislation allows it. And what about banks? They sit on troves of information that they are not using. Studies show they tag a mere 3 per cent of their data and analyse less than 0.5 per cent of it (Forrester, 2016). Considering regulations on data privacy, it comes as no surprise that selling data externally is not a viable route for holders of a banking licence. In fact, in some jurisdictions banking secrecy and data protection laws make it virtually impossible.

This does not mean data have to be locked in a vault, untouched by any employee. Banks can use them to up- and cross-sell their own financial products. This approach is a perfect booster to the white-label aggregation discussed earlier. If banks are the ones selling the products, there is no reason not to crunch data on customers' preferences. They can also use this data to improve the products in their portfolio. Google uses the texts people put into its translation tool to train its algorithm. Tesla collects every scrap of information to build its self-driving cars. Why shouldn't banks?

Complementors – the gold outside the pot

Cross-selling shows how profits loom in additional products and can balance the costs of a strong core offering. Selling more products is a never-ending challenge, but there is a way to lock users into more profitable products for good: complementors. While cross-selling means selling on top of the core offerings, complementors build on a contingency relationship; you cannot sell a blade without the customer having the corresponding razor, and you cannot sell Nespresso capsules without the customer having the machine. Only by having both products can you utilize the core product's potential. Due to this dependency, one of them can be offered at a very low price to serve as an entry point while the other drives profits (Grove, 1996). This is also known as the razor-and-blades model, and Brazilian Banco Original provides an example of how this works in banking. It grants its customers access to a bulk-buying platform where they can get particularly good prices. Banco Original leverages its capital resources and customer portfolio size to ensure quantity discounts, say a good car deal. With its many customers it is possible to mine data and find enough of them to bulk-buy a certain car model. The price advantages of these quantity purchases can then be passed down to the customer. Banco Original makes money by granting loans to finance the car. Cross-selling is still possible in this scenario – by selling car insurance, for example. Customers pay less for the car, but a higher interest on the loan (Stocco, 2015). Without the complementor, customers cannot profit from the bulk-buying advantage. Though, theoretically they could pay for the car with cash, this is unlikely. People bulk-buying a car are those who cannot afford to be picky about model, colour or features. Besides, it is easy to sift out customers who have the necessary cash in their accounts and not include them in the campaign – it is nothing more than simple customer segmentation.

Multiple other opportunities emerge with the blockchain. Think about smart contracts. Imagine after two years you want to sell the car you bought in the bulk-buying campaign. You never liked the model and only got it because it was a good bargain. You decide to sell it to your friend Eddie who cannot afford to pay for it all in one go, so you let him pay in instalments. But Eddie does not have a good track record in paying his debts so, to make sure he sticks to his commitment, you set up a blockchain-based smart contract whereby the car's doors only open if your account registers monthly payments until the amount is fully paid off. Or, to apply this to another scenario, you could decide to rent out your apartment and equip it with a smart lock that is controlled via a smart contract. Setting up smart contracts might be offered cheaply by your bank, with a monthly fee to cover the maintenance of the technical infrastructure in the background. In corporate banking, blockchain-based verification services

Setting up smart contracts might be offered cheaply by your bank.

could be chipped in while bloating prices for running an account, which would be a prerequisite for having access to the verification services.

Complementors have the potential to be the banks' strong point and, unlike fintechs, they have the necessary breadth in their portfolios to make it work. For data collectors, a complementor strategy is difficult to pull off. They already offer most services for free, making it hard to find 'blades' in a razor-and-blades model.

With this multitude of business models, which do you pick? The truth is, just as no strategy is inherently better or worse as we approach the blockchain age, neither is any business model. Rather, the choice is fuelled by the positioning and assets you have at your disposal. For differentiation-pursuing banks the fee-based or aggregator model works best, while for data collectors who lead their conquests with the cost-leadership approach it makes most sense to keep pushing their free-of-charge offers. Fintechs can go for the latter too, but due to their (initial) focus strategy the sub-models they choose can vary. Table 6.1 gives an overview of the business models that fit the various actor groups the best. Unfortunately, the table does not apply to all sub-actors within the main actor groups. Direct banks, for example, may use freemium models, though it generally is not recommended for banks. To make matters worse, B2B and B2C strategies might be carried out by the same companies but require different approaches. Also, some leading data behemoths have a hand in blockchain clouds, which blurs their positioning. For all these reasons the table is not dogmatic, but it still offers a general compass to start the strategy-building process.

TABLE 6.1 Strategic fit of business models and actor groups

Actors	Fee-based model	Aggregator model	Business model 'free'		
			Comple-mentors	Data aggrega-tion	Free-mium
Banks	High	High	High	Low	Low
Fintechs	Medium	Low	Low	Medium	High
Data-behemoths	Medium	Medium	Low	High	High

Globalized competition in a world of branding

Digitalization has jumbled the competitive intensity and the way companies make money. It will also add new arenas of competition – industries as well as geographies. The blockchain spells the erosion of national boundaries; its global ledger does not discriminate according to jurisdiction, and the costs are the same, whether you send money to your neighbour next door or to a web shop on another continent. Fintechs and data collectors already operate globally, and for banks it will become easier than ever before to do the same. In a truly globalized market there will be an unprecedented run by bigger banks to position themselves in countries all over the world. After all, once you have a blockchain system in place the set-up costs per country are a fraction of the level of investment currently required. The barrier ring-fencing the new markets is no longer the IT infrastructure but strong branding.

However, it does not necessarily follow that those with the biggest pockets will win the battle of the brands. Legacy problems plague marketing almost as much as they do IT. Current and past marketing approaches may, in fact, hold banks back from using their marketing budgets effectively. Though they have tremendous brand equity, it is fragmented and dispersed all over the world.

Many banks have dozens of brands for different markets, sometimes even multiple brands within one and the same country. This is more often than not the result of takeovers and local tweaking, as names are often chosen to reflect locality. The likes of Google and Amazon, however, transcend local preferences because they were built in a globalized and connected age. Fintechs are very much the same. PayPal might not have been a technical revolution, but the lesson its stellar rise teaches us is that a digital brand with global appeal can gain acceptance quickly, even in a non-emotion-arousing field such as finance. Global brands don't need to employ armies of marketers to mould the message into different logos, visual identities and word plays. If they want to sponsor international sports events, the effects will be wide-ranging as all countries will instantly recognize their brand. For banks, however, it is very unusual for local branches to be branded in the same way as international banking groups. Above all, IT giants own the interfaces customers look at every day; the Google lettering is seen every time someone searches the web, without costing Google a dime. The bitten-into Apple shines every time an iPad is lifted or an iMac is closed.

Though banks have tremendous brand equity, it is fragmented and dispersed all over the world.

Apart from brands, geographic proximity used to be the major reason why people chose a particular bank. This USP will no longer apply in a digitalized era, however. What banks need to do is to unify their appearance, concentrate their brand equity by absorbing local brands, and carve out a position in consumers' minds. Fidor Bank and some others are establishing themselves as a fresh alternative to dusty institutions. Yet banks will have to do more; they will have to find something unique that cannot be replicated – and something that scales. It is a tremendous upfront investment, and a risky endeavour, but one that will amortize over the years.

Creating a truly global brand does not just mean recolouring ads and corporate brochures. To be truly competitive globally you need to have the same positioning, the same messaging, but most importantly you will need to treat customers equally across all territories. It will be difficult to explain to a Chinese worker why they are paying higher account fees for a service than a student in the UK, or vice versa, or why a certain service is not offered in a certain territory.

Internationally strong brands leverage network effects. If the world is growing closer together and cross-border transactions are increasing, then a customer's payment method will be driven by what their international counterpart is able to accept. Is my counterpart using the same service, even though they are thousands of miles away? Are they aware of the brands and their offerings? The likelihood that users across borders both know and use the same financial brands is lower than both of them knowing Google, Facebook or Amazon, or even PayPal. This is why local social networks have not had much success; there are many local challengers to LinkedIn, for instance, but why would you bother with something that can only be used regionally when there is a global alternative? This is where a unified interface that could run all banks would help; a SWIFT-like cooperation, perhaps?

Competition is always good. It is good for customer service, good for prices and good for innovativeness.

So blockchain is set to break down national barriers, which is a welcomed effect. Competition is always good. It is good for customer service, good for prices and good for innovativeness. Globalized competition is even better. With fewer boundaries and more service providers to choose from, prices will tumble, and the lower prices go the less economic inequality there will be. Over centuries the free-market principle has been the largest equalizing force in the world. The blockchain is its latest expansion, because cutting prices on capital and payments has a particularly accelerating effect. In Chapter 7 we will consider whether or not this will play out, and how it might do so.

CHAPTER SEVEN

An Unparalleled Promise… for Some

Myth: 'The blockchain will erode the gap between the haves and have nots.'

Unleashing the free market by unbinding capital

Like any technological breakthrough, the blockchain has triggered numerous discussions about its ethical impact. Thanks to its numerous application possibilities there are many horrifying ethical dangers, but to counterbalance these there are also exhilarating possibilities. For payments, there are four broad themes when considering the ethical dimensions of the blockchain: fuelling the shadow economy, slashing traditional jobs, pumping up the legitimate economy, and creating global financial equality.

Let us look at the first one. The fact that blockchain can be used for shady business has captured the public's attention like no other topic. Regarded rather soberly, this is not the most ethically impactful dimension, but there are examples of how the blockchain can be used as a force for good in this regard. Just think about the Silk Road crackdown mentioned earlier. The underlying question is always how much government control is necessary and desirable. Bitcoins make it very hard for authorities to track illegal activities, ranging from the funding of terrorists and money laundering to ordering hacking attacks in the deep web. At the same time, however, they enable the funding of independent media in autocratic regimes. Bitcoin's proponents defend it by arguing that it is not the flaws in the technology that nurture its dark side, but 'abuse by people' (Umeh, 2016). They are right in that cash can just as well be used as an instrument for illegal activities, but there is evidence of an extreme correlation between bitcoin and underground markets (Christin, 2013). If banks manage to harness the technology and squeeze it into the corset of current regulation, all the bad aftertaste of the deep web would be swallowed and blockchain could become a force for good. For this to happen, banks need to legitimize it. Again, the silver bullet is centralized blockchains, as the technical set-up allows for all necessary controls. This is not to say, however, that bitcoin and other decentralized applications should be banned. Canada's light-touch approach discussed in Chapter 2 is a better way to deal with the problem. You cannot control everything on the dark side of the net, but governments must eliminate the possibility of 'dirty' crypto value being brought into the legal system. They could do this by regulating exchanges or even giving them licences, as well as tracking and analysing monetary movements.

The second criticism of the blockchain, that it will slash traditional jobs, cannot be dealt with by regulation. For most of human history, extraordinary economic growth has correlated with automation but, at the same time, automation has had a negative impact on employment levels in the fields it revolutionized. So it is no wonder there is concern about the impact that blockchain could have on current finance jobs. This criticism is levelled against any new technology, be it driverless cars or web shops, but at the end of the day, innovation frees up capacities that can be directed elsewhere. There are more than enough capacities to make use of: in the United States alone 6.2 million people work in finance (SelectUSA, 2016), whilst in the UK it is 1.1 million (MacAskill, Jessop and Cohn, 2017). Is there really an observable technology impact on employment numbers, however, or is it just a figment promulgated by jittery journalists and trade-union barons?

Let's have a look at comparable breakthroughs in the past. The ATM is perhaps the best example of a banking technology that made human labour obsolete. Before its introduction, clerks and tellers used to perform monotonous tasks: checking IDs and account balances, counting money and meticulously documenting each transaction. It is worth recalling the Citicorp example from Chapter 3 and looking at the ATM's impact on its workforce. The actual figures speak volumes: when Citicorp introduced the magic machines, the number of branch employees did not plummet. On the contrary: it went from 7,100 in 1977 to 8,400 in 1988. How was that possible? The new technology replaced handing over bills with more challenging tasks such as up- and cross-selling products. Moreover, the ATM gave Citicorp an unseen edge over competition. Customers were not only won over from competitors, but people who previously had not made very much use of banking services – perhaps because they eschewed personal contact – actually visited the bank more often. The market was enlarged (Glaser, 1988) and employees were happier as minuscule duties were replaced by more demanding ones.

When Citicorp introduced ATMs, the number of branch employees did not plummet.

However, the blockchain will also have a positive ethical impact, in that it is expected to pump up the legitimate economy and foster global financial equality. According to forecasts, the blockchain will save banks $15–20 billion yearly (Santander, Oliver Wyman and Anthemis

Group, 2015). This cash will then be invested to fuel other parts of the economy. In investment banking, the technology reduces the transaction lifespan, thus freeing up massive capital that is currently blocked to back trades until they are settled. Blockchain also enables easy microloans that will pump fresh and immediate capital directly into the market. By 2025, Foundation Capital (2014) reckons that crowdfunding and P2P lending will reach a volume of US $1 trillion, and to a large degree this will only be made possible by the blockchain. When this cash is reinvested or spent, it will trigger a wave of economic growth. In a way, it is comparable to the invention of the joint-stock company or credit creation. Every time vast sums of cash are freed up, an economic boom follows. More money is invested into industry, technology, and research and development, which, in turn, eventually raises quality of life for everyone.

If accounts and transfers get cheaper, the assumption must be that financial equality will rise.

So economies will become richer and, as this happens, and more people have access to affordable banking services, we can expect the number of the unbanked to fall. New segments of the population will gain access to banking services and thus improve their personal finances. Nevertheless, growth in the mature Western markets will soon hit the ceiling. Regions previously frowned upon from a risk and revenue side might prove to be the new Promised Land.

The largest market expansion in history – onboarding the two billion unbanked

So there is potential for blockchain to have a bright future in developing countries; it can offer a parallel structure to defy oppressive regimes, a way to move money in regions without banks, and all at a fraction of the current price. In fact, the so-called bitcoin market potential index (Hileman, 2015), a measure quantifying the chances of bitcoin's success according to country, ranks Argentina, Venezuela and many Sub-Saharan countries at the top of the list. Steady inflation, financial crises and a vibrant shady economy are the main drivers. Amidst these problems, radical groups – the best known is Bitnation – even dream of replacing state monopolies by distributed ledgers and smart contracts.

But let us look at the facts. So far only anecdotal evidence exists that people are using bitcoins. Why? For starters, the potential of capturing the unbanked is hysterically inflated. Having a smartphone is not enough; not all of those 1 billion unbanked smartphone users (Rangan and Lee, 2010) can run the necessary applications, because they mostly use refurbished and outdated hardware. Also, cryptocurrencies are not easy to use and there is very little awareness of them in the world's poorer regions. For those who are aware, the fear of losing everything through cyber theft or an exchange going bankrupt might hold them back. Even if, by some miracle, you could make all of the unbanked use bitcoins and spirit away all the deficiencies of the cryptocurrency, the equalizing impact would be disillusioning. Why? Because bitcoin and other decentralized cryptocurrency start-ups are weakest in what is needed the most for financial inclusion: credit. Being able to move around money is great but it doesn't help you if you don't have anything to move around in the first place. To be able to offer credit, you need liquidity, risk experts and stability mechanisms – an algorithm alone will not cut it. P2P lending will help, but it has limits.

So obviously, these quick fixes to societal problems are not what they might first appear. Bitcoin will abolish poverty as much as smart contracts will abolish tyranny. I shall therefore focus on what banks and data collectors can do with fiat currencies that are powered by blockchain as a back-end engine. This will enable slow but substantial improvement.

There is enormous potential, but it will just take longer than expected. Around 2 billion adults are currently locked out of the financial system (World Bank Group, 2015). Some choose this but most people do not have any other option; either the infrastructure is not available or it is so expensive that only a select few can afford it. While a rift does persist between banked and unbanked people in the United States and Europe, really it is a problem in developing countries, where only 51 per cent of the population have an account compared to 94 per cent in OECD countries (World Bank Group, 2015). What aggravates the situation is that US and European banks are increasingly shunning international markets, even pulling out of them. Consider how Citi is offloading businesses outside the United States. It had 50 foreign affiliates in 2007. Ten years later 19 were left. Its European counterparts have been lopping off dependencies at the same pace. Chinese banks are showing an opposite trend (*The Economist*, 2017), but whether they can make up for the Euro–US retrenchment that exacerbates the economic imbalance among countries is questionable. Yes, being overbanked does not lead to poverty; being underbanked does – this is a simple lesson that many crypto enthusiasts have yet to learn. When there are no legitimate financial institutions, people cannot safeguard their possessions, do not have resources to invest, and eventually shady loan sharks fill the void. They collect stifling interest rates that inevitably cause people to default, and, as loan sharks operate illegally, these defaults can have terrifying consequences for the customer; it is no coincidence that in most people's heads they conjure up pictures of debtors being beaten or their thumbs cut off. Illegitimate sources of capital worsen the divide between the haves and have-nots, and they enable and are enabled by an entire network of organized crime that grows in the absence of

Being overbanked does not lead to poverty; being underbanked does.

a legitimate alternative. So only once financial inequality drops can economic inequality do the same. Taxes from capital value-creation flow into the treasury and the rule of law and order are strengthened.

Financial vacuums, however, do not always have to be filled by grim, torturing debt collectors. The lack of an effective financial market can slow down the economic process by depriving people of security and funds. In regions where institutions exist, but face little competition, exorbitant fees and interest blossom, which in turn crimp economic growth as people hesitate to use the services. This is where the blockchain could help. By cutting to the bone the cost of storing and transferring money, access to financial services should explode, raising the standard of living and contributing to more equality within an economy. This equality will, in turn, fuel macroeconomic growth and trim the gap between countries.

There is another cash injection that poorer economies will get from the blockchain, as it will lower the currently horrendous remittance costs. Contrary to popular belief, the largest flow of money from the West into developing countries is not foreign aid. It is not direct foreign investment, either, but remittances that diasporas send back home. In Haiti, for example, in 2015, 25 per cent of the gross domestic product (GDP) was made up of remittances; in the Philippines it was around 10 per cent (FRED, 2017a, 2017b). It is quite common to pay fees of up to 7 per cent because the money is tied up for weeks before it reaches its destination. One example of how blockchain can eliminate those fees and free up capital immediately is the start-up Abra. It uses bitcoin and Litecoin, a closely related cryptocurrency, to turn every smartphone into a cash teller for other members of the network. Yet without fiat currencies remittance solutions face an additional challenge: they need sufficiently liquid currency markets. Again, slashing remittances is only a patch that can stop *some* money bleeding from the financial system. What developing countries need more is a systematic overhaul on all levels: transacting, storing and lending. This will not happen if fiat currencies and banks continue to be categorically rejected by the blockchain community.

The threat of banking deserts and local divides

So the outlook is simple: as blockchain makes financial services cheaper banks can grab billions of new customers and thus lift left-behind regions out of poverty and despair. Unfortunately, this scenario relies on another common misconception: that blockchain transactions are free. Here I am not just talking about bitcoin transactions – although their price has been shooting through the roof; in mid-December 2017 the average bitcoin transaction cost US $28 (Browne, 2017). I am also talking about efficient centralized solutions. Solving algorithms to verify transactions gobbles energy and relies on IT infrastructure that needs to be set up and serviced. This all costs money. Despite this, however, the myth of free blockchain transactions still persists.

The costs far transcend the technical: fighting money laundering and terrorism financing, obeying economic sanctions, and making the brand and offering known to customers all require money to be pumped into a market relentlessly. The costs of regional expansion far outweigh those for other famous IT solutions that have recently played an equalizing role – say Google's search engine. Don't forget, banks want to *make* money. Wait, what about the free basic services I presented earlier as a viable business model? The crucial point is that these rely on some sort of cross- or up-selling – the banks do not make their money from fees attached to bank accounts, but from loans and insurance policies. These things are very hard to sell where there is little purchasing power, and if there is little potential to cross-sell profitable products, why would anyone bother building and maintaining the free offering in the first place? The fact that high-risk products such as credit and insurance are more expensive for the customer in poorer regions weakens the case even further. The simple fact is that banks need to earn much more money to allow for the high default rate; it is much more likely that people will be unable to pay their dues than it is in a strong economy. This inevitably means that interest rates will look worse in Somalia than in Sweden.

Naturally, banks pivot to serve more profitable regions, thereby leaving behind a vacuum known as 'banking deserts'. These are wide stretches of land where the population has no or limited access to financial services. In Chapter 5 we saw the devastating long-term effect that bank branch closures can have not only on private individuals, but also on small and medium-sized enterprises. The competitive intensity among banks is inextricably interwoven with the economic health of a region. Even milder forms of deserts, with one or two institutions, make it harder and more expensive for people to get their hands on cash. Often local players offer only high-margin services, hampering growth. Payday lending, for example, is more expensive than longer-term loans. But in the face of lacking alternatives, people have to resort to this interest-heavy credit.

So eventually, the blockchain could have a similar effect as the introduction of mega-stores: in spite of providing cheaper services, entire segments deemed unprofitable run the risk of not being serviced. In this scenario, the cost advantages will be passed on to customers in regions with many competitors. Ergo, groups already better off see their costs fall while those struggling do not. So instead of alleviating inequality, blockchain's cost-slashing could actually exacerbate it.

In poor countries deserts are larger, more frequent, and have a bigger impact due to other missing infrastructure. When highways are decrepit and gas is expensive, jumping into your car to visit a bank branch 100 miles away just to get an extension on your mortgage payment is not really a viable option. This danger is not limited to small African villages cut off from the urban centres, however. Take the example of the United States. Nearly

20 per cent of all households are underbanked, and 7 per cent are completely unbanked. They are more likely to be non-white, have little formal education and earn less. In addition to this, a disproportionally high 10 per cent of those households have sent remittances in the past 12 months, thus paying especially high fees. Lower-income households are already burdened with financial expenses far more than the upper echelons of the income curve. Is it any wonder, then, that 27.7 per cent of unbanked respondents say a major reason they do not have an account is because it is too expensive? The fear of high or unpredictable fees also features prominently for 24 per cent of the respondents (FDIC, 2016).

The widening gap powers a negative spiral. The more money you pay for financial services and the more your purchasing power edges down, the less attractive you become in the eyes of financial actors. This in turn leads to stagnant or even higher prices. The exciting thing about spirals, however, is that they can be turned the other way around too. So the blockchain could make use of an inbuilt acceleration effect: the more the purchasing power increases, the more attractive the unbanked segments become and the more access they gain to capital. So the blockchain will be a catalyst of equalization, but it will be a treacherous path, and quite different to how proponents imagine it will be. It will also depend on a host of other factors as it is part of a bundle of technologies, such as artificial intelligence or big data, that make up the digital paradigm. Blockchain is the key that will ultimately unlock the potential of digital banking and smartphone penetration.

Rays of hope

Over the course of history, financial revolutions have shaped humankind, often preceding radical societal and technological changes. As we saw at the beginning of this book, this was the case for the development of the written word that was invented to keep track of monetary transactions. It was also the case for the Industrial Revolution in Britain and Europe, for which three major financial innovations in the 17th century paved the way: intra- and inter-bank transactions constituted the first breakthrough. With them, branches were able to send money to an entire network of financial institutions, instead of limiting their customers to one bank only. The Amsterdam Exchange Bank (Wisselbank) allowed merchants to credit someone else's account by debiting their own. However, the bank could only give out money it actually stacked in the vault. Although this prevented the possibility of a bank run, ie the bank running out of cash due to all its customers withdrawing their money simultaneously, it meant banks could not perform what would later become known as 'fractional reserve banking' or simply 'credit creation'. Credit creation, the second big breakthrough, was introduced in the middle of the 17th century. This was when banks lent out deposits from other borrowers. This injected unseen mountains of cash into the economy and allowed for the investments needed in order for the Industrial Revolution to take place. The third game changer was the creation of the Bank of England, which became the first bank with a monopoly to issue notes. This was a classic central bank (Ferguson, 2008). You now may ask yourself why does all of this matter? Why is financial history important to the blockchain? Quite simply, because it illustrates how every time finance evolves, people's lives improve. The availability of capital is crucial to allow all other sectors of the economy and society to blossom. Regardless of the paradigm that holds sway, and regardless of the primary resource driving its growth, the availability and flows of money decide just how effective the paradigm can be. Data might be the oil of the 21st century, but the need for capital never

Data might be the oil of the 21st century, but the need for capital never changes.

changes; it is a constant, the grease of the human progress machine. Today its circulation makes sure that data can be collected, stored and analysed properly, just as in the past it made sure oil could be dug up, refined and transported to its destination.

Blockchain enthusiasts see their technology conquering every pore of human life, but the truth is that it does not have to do this in order to make a difference. Most people will see a benefit if all it does is enhance the financial system. Does it seem far-fetched that the lessons from the invention of writing or the Industrial Revolution can be transferred to cryptography and distributed computing? Fair enough, but then take a look at what a financial innovation far less revolutionary than the blockchain can do. Remember the Kenyan SMS payment system M-Pesa? A study about it published in *Science* found that the access to mobile money sent the number of households in poverty down by 192,000 (or 2 per cent) and fuelled long-term consumption. In addition to this, it had an equalizing gender-effect as it was particularly female-led households that profited from M-Pesa (Suri and Jack, 2016) – 192,000 within one country is a lot of people. Augmenting finance and thereby economics has a transforming effect on a society far larger than any insular solution. The blockchain may well be an immutable ledger that the land register can be put on to, but there is no point doing this if an autocratic regime has a lock on the power. Heaving hundreds of thousands or even millions of people out of poverty and docking them to the financial system is a different story. It gives them more options, more economic heft, and eventually more political power. The finance impact is the basic blockchain benefit upon which all others are built. It will not come overnight, but it will come. Its effect will be sustainable and embedded into the digital paradigm like all of the previous financial innovations were embedded into their paradigms.

For this to play out, the focus must be on what the blockchain is really about. The title of this book draws a parallel between the blockchain and the Tower of Babel. This is an allusion to a 'confusion of tongues' resulting from the hubris that has accompanied the new technology. Blockchain is mixed up with its applications, bitcoin is hyped despite being technically doomed, mechanisms and terminology are confused, and every walk of human life is putatively equally ripe for disruption. Seven big myths hang like dark clouds over each discussion, myths that have been debunked throughout the course of this book. Through all the shouting at conferences and in the media, and the catchphrases that dominate the headlines, it is difficult to discern those initiatives that will really make a difference.

The blockchain might just be the technology to unlock the showdown between two groups of goliaths, a showdown that has already started in East Asia: banks versus data behemoths. And a showdown it will be. Digital giants and start-ups alike have conquered one industry after another, but their winning streak came to a halt when they faced competitors of their own calibre. Amazon conquered many retail segments, but so far they have not been successful with groceries, because Walmart is a behemoth equal in heft and efficiency. Not displacing the 'Beast of Bentonville' like incumbents from other industries displayed the limits of Silicon Valley's perceived omnipotence. Expect a similarly exciting battle with the banks. Data behemoths will not meet passive resistance, but giants with unconquerable fortresses and a war chest sizeable enough to be envied by every other industry. In the end, it is not their existence that it is at stake, but their market share.

The blockchain might just be the technology to unlock the showdown between two groups of goliaths: banks versus data behemoths.

So if you happen to be a general embroiled in this battle, remember that data behemoths have been so successful because of their customer-centricity. So has Walmart. It managed to defy them because of its size, but first and foremost because it does more than to put customers first – it puts them at the centre of everything it does. Banks also have to learn to revolve around the customer, not the regulator or compliance officer. They have to adapt all of their processes – front-end *and* back-end – to fit their customers' needs.

If you are not at the front line, but just an interested spectator, then sit back and enjoy the ride. Because among all the uncertainties, one thing is for sure: *you* will be on the winning side as the competitive forces of the free market push down the cost of banking services. The more intense the battle gets, the more you will enjoy it.

References

Introduction

Ali, R *et al* (2014) Innovations in payment technologies and the emergence of digital currencies, *Bank of England Quarterly Bulletin*, Q3, pp 1–14

Bovaird, C (2016) [accessed 15 February 2018] Bitcoin Price Climbs Over 50% in First Half of 2016, *CoinDesk*, 12/07 [Online] http://www.CoinDesk.com/bitcoin-price-h1-report-2016/

Burne, K and Sidel, R (2017) [accessed 15 February 2018] Hackers Ran Through Holes in Swift's Network: Payment-Transfer Network Left Banks Largely Responsible For Their Own Cyberdefense; Old Passwords at Bangladesh's Central Bank, *The Wall Street Journal*, 30/04 [Online] https://www.wsj.com/articles/hackers-ran-through-holes-in-swifts-network-1493575442

Coinometrics (2015) in Skinner, C (2016) *Value Web: How fintech firms are using mobile and blockchain technologies to create the internet of value*, Marshall Cavendish Business, Singapore

Dimon, J (2015) [accessed 20 August 2018] JP Morgan Chase & Co, Annual Report 2014 [Online] http://files.shareholder.com/downloads/ONE/15660259x0x820077/8af78e45-1d81-4363-931c-439d04312ebc/JPMC-AR2014-LetterToShareholders.pdf

Donnelly, J (2016) [accessed 15 February 2018] Why Bitcoin's Halving Was a Boring Vindication, *Coindesk*, 16/07 [Online] http://www.CoinDesk.com/bitcoin-halving-event-boring-vindication-software/

Eyal, I and Gün Sirer, E (2014) [accessed 15 February 2018] Majority Is Not Enough: Bitcoin Mining is Vulnerable, *The 18th International Conference on Financial Cryptography and Data Security (FC), Barbados* [Online] https://arxiv.org/abs/1311.0243

Franco, P (2015) *Understanding Bitcoin: Cryptography, engineering and economics*, Wiley Finance Series, Chichester

Heires, K (2016) The risks and rewards of blockchain technology, *Risk Management* (March), pp 4–7

Hertig, A (2018) [accessed 15 February 2018] How To Save On Bitcoin's Soaring Fees, *CoinDesk*, 23/01 [Online] https://www.coindesk.com/save-bitcoins-soaring-fees/

Hileman, G (2016) [accessed 15 February 2018] State of Bitcoin and Blockchain 2016, *CoinDesk*, 01/02 [Online] http://www.CoinDesk.com/state-of-bitcoin-blockchain-2016/

Kaminska, I (2014) [accessed 15 February 2018] Bitcoin's Wasted Power – and How It Could Be Used to Heat Homes, *Financial Times*, 05/09 [Online] https://www.ft.com/content/384a349a-32a5-11e4-93c6-00144feabdc0

Leising, M (2015) [accessed 15 February 2018] The Blockchain Revolution Gets Endorsement in Wall Street Survey, *Bloomberg News*, 22/07 [Online] http://www.bloomberg.com/news/articles/2015-07-22/the-blockchain-revolution-gets-endorsement-in-wall-street-survey

McCook, H (2014) [accessed 15 February 2018] Under the Microscope: Economic and Environmental Costs of Bitcoin Mining, *CoinDesk*, 21/06 [Online] http://www.CoinDesk.com/microscope-economic-environmental-costs-bitcoin-mining/

Nakamoto, S (2008) [accessed 15 February 2018] Bitcoin: A Peer-to-Peer Electronic Cash System [Online] https://bitcoin.org/bitcoin.pdf

Peters, G and Panayi, E (2015) [accessed 15 February 2018] Understanding Modern Banking Ledgers through Blockchain Technologies: Future of Transaction Processing and Smart Contracts on the Internet of Money, *Cornell University*, 18/11 [Online] https://arxiv.org/pdf/1511.05740.pdf

Santander InnoVentures, Oliver Wyman and Anthemis (2015) [accessed 15 February 2018] The Fintech 2.0 Paper: Rebooting Financial Services [Online] http://santanderinnoventures.com/wp-content/uploads/2015/06/The-Fintech-2-0-Paper.pdf

Skinner, C (2016) *Value Web: How fintech firms are using mobile and blockchain technologies to create the internet of value*, Marshall Cavendish Business, Singapore

Swan, M (2015) *Blockchain: Blueprint for a new economy*, O'Reilly Media Inc, Sebastopol, CA

Tapscott, D and Tapscott, A (2016) *Blockchain Revolution: How the technology behind bitcoin is changing money, business, and the world*, Penguin Random House, New York

The Economist (2015) Briefing blockchains: the great chain of being sure about things, *The Economist*, 31/10, pp 21–24

The Economist (2016) [accessed 15 February 2018] The World If – If Financial Systems Were Hacked, *The Economist*, 16/6 [Online] http://worldif.economist.com/article/12136/joker-pack

The Economist (2017) [accessed 15 February 2018] Why Everything Is Hackable: Computer Security Is Broken From Top To Bottom, *The Economist*, 08/04 [Online] https://www.economist.com/news/science-and-technology/21720268-consequences-pile-up-things-are-starting-improve-computer-security

The Nilson Report (2017) [accessed 15 February 2018] Card Fraud Losses Reach $22.80 Billion, *The Nilson Report*, 1118 (October) [Online] https://www.nilsonreport.com/publication_the_current_issue.php

Umeh, J (2016) Blockchain: Double Bubble or Double Trouble, *ITNOW* (March), pp. 58–61

Walport, M (2016) [accessed 15 February 2018] Distributed Ledger Technology: Beyond Block Chain – A Report by the UK Government Chief Scientific Adviser [Online] https://www.gov.uk/government/uploads/system/uploads/attachment_data/file/492972/gs-16-1-distributed-ledger-technology.pdf

Wild, J, Arnold, M and Stafford, P (2015) [accessed 15 February 2018] Technology: Banks Seek the Key to Blockchain: Financial Groups Race to Harness the Power of the Bitcoin Infrastructure to Slash Costs, *Financial Times*, 1/11 [Online] https://next.ft.com/content/eb1f8256-7b4b-11e5-a1fe-567b37f80b64

Wile, R (2013) [accessed 15 February 2018] 927 People Own Half of Bitcoin, *Business Insider*, 10/12 [Online] http://www.businessinsider.com/927-people-own-half-of-the-bitcoins-2013-12?IR=T

Chapter 1

Ali, R *et al* (2014) Innovations in payment technologies and the emergence of digital currencies, *Bank of England Quarterly Bulletin*, Q3, pp 1–14

Baxendale, G (2016) Can Blockchain Revolutionise ERPs?, *ITNOW* (March), pp 38–39

Chaum, D (1983) Blind signatures for untraceable payments, *Advances in Cryptology Proceedings*, **82** (3), pp 199–203

Christensen, C (1997) *The Innovator's Dilemma: When technologies cause great firms to fail*, Harvard Business School Press, Boston, MA

Coinmarketcap (2018) [accessed 15 February 2018] Cryptocurrency Market Capitalizations [Online] https://coinmarketcap.com/currencies/ethereum/

Danneels, E (2004) Disruptive technology reconsidered: a critique and research agenda, *Journal of Product Innovation Management*, **21**, pp 246–58

eMarketer (2016) [accessed 15 February 2018] Worldwide Retail eCommerce Sales Will Reach $1.915 Trillion This Year [Online] https://www.emarketer.com/Article/Worldwide-Retail-Ecommerce-Sales-Will-Reach-1915-Trillion-This-Year/1014369

European Commission [accessed 15 February 2018] Factsheet on the 'Right To Be Forgotten' Ruling (C-131/12) [Online] http://ec.europa.eu/justice/data-protection/files/factsheets/factsheet_data_protection_en.pdf

Franco, P (2014) *Understanding Bitcoin: Cryptography, engineering and economics*, John Wiley & Sons, Chichester

Freeman, C (1982) *The Economics of Industrial Innovation*, Frances Pinter, London

Freeman, C (1987) *Technology Policy and Economic Performance: Lessons From Japan*, Pinter, London

Freeman, C and Perez, C (1988) Structural crisis of adjustment: business cycles and investment behaviour, in *Technical Change and Economic Theory*, ed G Dosi *et al*, pp 38–66, Frances Pinter, London

Gartner (2015) [accessed 15 February 2018] *Gartner, IoT Report, November 2015*, Press release from 10 November 2015, Gartner Says 6.4 Billion Connected 'Things' Will Be In Use In 2016, Up 30 Percent From 2015 [Online] http://www.gartner.com/newsroom/id/3165317

Hileman, G (2016) [accessed 15 February 2018] State of Bitcoin and Blockchain 2016, *CoinDesk*, 01/02 [Online] http://www.CoinDesk.com/state-of-bitcoin-blockchain-2016/

Internet World Stats (2017) [accessed 15 February 2018] Internet Usage Statistics: The Internet Big Picture [Online] http://www.internetworldstats.com/stats.htm

Intuit (2012) [accessed 15 February 2018] GoPayment Survey Estimates $100 Billion in Missed Sales for Small Businesses that Deny Plastic,

Investor Relations, 22/05 [Online] http://investors.intuit.com/Press-Releases/Press-Release-Details/2012/GoPayment-Survey-Estimates-100-Billion-in-Missed-Sales-for-Small-Businesses-that-Deny-Plastic/default.aspx

Kiesnoski, K (2017) [accessed 15 February 2018] The Top 10 US Companies by Market Capitalization, *CNBC*, 24/10 [Online] https://www.cnbc.com/2017/03/08/the-top-10-us-companies-by-market-capitalization.html

Kulaev, S (2015) [accessed 15 February 2018] Nearly Half of Mortgage Borrowers Don't Shop Around When They Buy a Home, *Consumer Financial Protection Bureau*, 13/01 [Online] https://www.consumerfinance.gov/about-us/blog/nearly-half-of-mortgage-borrowers-dont-shop-around-when-they-buy-a-home/

McKinsey (2017) [accessed 15 February 2018] Payments: On the Crest of the Fintech Wave, *Report May* [Online] https://www.mckinsey.com/industries/financial-services/our-insights/payments-on-the-crest-of-the-fintech-wave

NASDAQ (2016) [accessed 15 February 2018] Building on the Blockchain, *MarketInsite*, 23/03 [Online] http://business.nasdaq.com/marketinsite/2016/Building-on-the-Blockchain.html

Oliver Wyman and Euroclear (2016) [accessed 15 February 2018] Blockchain in Capital Markets: The Prize and the Journey, *Report*, February [Online] http://www.oliverwyman.com/content/dam/oliver-wyman/global/en/2016/feb/BlockChain-In-Capital-Markets.pdf

Peachey, K (2017) [accessed 15 February 2018] Mobiles 'Fast Replacing' Bank Branch Visits, *BBC*, 28/06 [Online] http://www.bbc.com/news/business-40421868

Perez, C (2009) Technological revolutions and techno-economic paradigms, *Working Papers in Technology Governance and Economic Dynamics*, **20**, pp 1–16

Peters, G, Chapelle, A and Panayi, E (2014) [accessed 15 February 2018] Opening Discussion on Banking Sector Risk Exposures and Vulnerabilities from Virtual Currencies: An Operational Risk Perspective [Online] https://arxiv.org/ftp/arxiv/papers/1409/1409.1451.pdf

Pilcher, J (2017) [accessed 15 February 2018] Branches in Decline: Last One Out, Turn Off the Lights, *The Financial Brand*, 11/07 [Online] https://thefinancialbrand.com/66228/bank-credit-union-branch-traffic/

Pureswaran, V and Brody, P (2015) [accessed 15 February 2018] Device Democracy: Saving the Future of the Internet of Things, *IBM Report* [Online] http://www-935.ibm.com/services/multimedia/GBE03620USEN.pdf

Santander InnoVentures, Oliver Wyman and Anthemis (2015) [accessed 15 February 2018] The Fintech 2.0 Paper: Rebooting Financial Services [Online] http://santanderinnoventures.com/wp-content/uploads/2015/06/The-Fintech-2-0-Paper.pdf

Skinner, C (2016) [accessed 15 February 2018] *Value Web: How FinTech firms are using mobile and blockchain technologies to create the internet of value*, Marshall Cavendish Business, Singapore

Statista (2017) PayPal – Statistics & Facts [Online] https://www.statista.com/topics/2411/paypal/

Swan, M (2015) [accessed 15 February 2018] *Blockchain: Blueprint for a new economy*, O'Reilly Media Inc, Sebastopol, CA

Szabo, N (1997) [accessed 15 February 2018] Formalizing and Securing Relationships on Public Networks, *First Monday*, **2** (9) [Online] http://firstmonday.org/article/view/548/469

Tapscott, D and Tapscott, A (2016) *Blockchain Revolution: How the technology behind bitcoin is changing money, business, and the world*, Penguin Random House, New York

The Economist (2015) Briefing blockchains: the great chain of being sure about things, *The Economist*, 31/10, pp 21–24

The Economist (2017) [accessed 15 February 2018] For American Express, Competition Will Only Intensify: As Kenneth Chenault Departs, What Does the Future Hold for Amex? *The Economist*, 28/10 [Online] https://www.economist.com/news/finance-and-economics/21730639-kenneth-chenault-departs-what-does-future-hold-amex-american

The Nilson Report (2017a) [accessed 15 February 2018] POS Terminal Shipments Worldwide, *The Nilson Report*, 1114 (July) [Online] https://www.nilsonreport.com/publication_newsletter_archive_issue.php?issue=1114

The Nilson Report (2017b) [accessed 15 February 2018] Card Fraud Losses Reach $22.80 Billion, *The Nilson Report*, 1118 (October) [Online] https://www.nilsonreport.com/publication_the_current_issue.php

Tushman, M and Anderson, P (1986) Technological discontinuities and organizational environment, *Administrative Science Quarterly*, **1** (3), pp 429–65

Walport, M (2016) [accessed 15 February 2018] Distributed Ledger Technology: Beyond Block Chain – A Report by the UK Government Chief Scientific Adviser [Online] https://www.gov.uk/government/uploads/system/uploads/attachment_data/file/492972/gs-16-1-distributed-ledger-technology.pdf

Chapter 2

Biryukov, A, Khovratovich, D and Pustogarov, I (2014) [accessed 15 February 2018] Deanonymisation of Clients in Bitcoin P2P Network, *Proc. 2014 ACM SIGSAC Conf. Computer and Communication Security*, pp 15–29 [Online] https://arxiv.org/pdf/1405.7418.pdf

Brennan, S (2018) [accessed 15 February 2018] Contortions for Compliance: Life Under New York's BitLicense, *Coindesk*, 21/01 [Online] https://www.coindesk.com/contortions-compliance-life-new-yorks-bitlicense/

Brito, J and Castillo, A (2013) [accessed 15 February 2018] Bitcoin: A Primer for Policymakers, *Mercatus Center (George Mason University)* [Online] https://www.mercatus.org/system/files/Brito_BitcoinPrimer.pdf

Canadian Senate (2015) [accessed 15 February 2018] Digital Currency: You Can't Flip This Coin, *Report on the Standing Committee on Banking, Trade and Commerce* [Online] https://sencanada.ca/content/sen/Committee/412/banc/rep/rep12jun15-e.pdf

Coinmarketcap (2018) [accessed 15 February 2018] Cryptocurrency Market Capitalizations [Online] https://coinmarketcap.com/currencies/

Decker, S and Surane, J (2018) [accessed 15 February 2018] BofA Tops IBM, Payments Firms With Most Blockchain Patents, *Bloomberg*, 16/01 [Online] https://www.bloomberg.com/news/articles/2018-01-16/bofa-tops-ibm-and-payments-firms-with-most-blockchain-patents

Desjardins, J (2015) [accessed 15 February 2018] All of the World's Money and Markets in One Visualization, *The Money Project*, 17/12 [Online] http://money.visualcapitalist.com/all-of-the-worlds-money-and-markets-in-one-visualization/?link=mktw

Deutsche Bank (2016) [accessed 15 February 2018] White Paper: FinTech 2.0: Creating New Opportunities through Strategic Alliance, *White Paper*, February [Online] http://cib.db.com/insights-and-initiatives/white-papers/FinTech_2_0_Creating_new_opportunities_through_strategic_alliance.htm

Euro Banking Association (2015) [accessed 15 February 2018] Cryptotechnologies, a Major IT Innovation and Catalyst for Change: 4 Categories, 4 Applications and 4 Scenarios: An Exploration for Transaction Banking and Payment Professionals, *Report*, 11/05 [Online] http://www.the-blockchain.com/docs/Euro%20Banking%20Association%20-%20Cryptotechnologies%20-%20%20a%20major%20IT%20innovation.pdf

Ferguson, N (2008) *The Ascent of Money: A financial history of the world*, Penguin Books, London

Goodhart, C (1988) *The Evolution of Central Banks*, MIT Press, Cambridge, MA

Hileman, G (2016) [accessed 15 February 2018] State of Bitcoin and blockchain 2016, *CoinDesk*, 01/02 [Online] http://www.CoinDesk.com/state-of-bitcoin-blockchain-2016/

Jones, G and Hill, C (2012) *Theory of Strategic Management*, South-Western CENGAGE Learning

Kharif, O (2014) [accessed 15 February 2018] Bitcoin: Not Just for Libertarians and Anarchists Anymore: Bitcoin Draws Consumers and Businesses Even as its Value Slides, *Bloomberg Business*, 9/10 [Online] https://www.bloomberg.com/news/articles/2014-10-09/bitcoin-not-just-for-libertarians-and-anarchists-anymore

MacMillan, I and McGrath, R (2000) Technology Strategy in Lumpy Market Landscapes, in *Wharton on Managing Emerging Technologies*, ed G Day, P Shoemaker and R Gunther, pp 150–71, Wiley, New York

Möser, M, Böhme, R and Breuker, D (2013) An inquiry into the money laundering tools in the bitcoin ecosystem, *Proceedings of the 2013 eCrime Researchers Summit,* IEEE

Nikkei (2017) [accessed 15 February 2018] Japan-South Korea Blockchain Payments Enter Trials Friday, *Asian Review*, 13/12 [Online] https://asia.nikkei.com/Business/Deals/Japan-South-Korea-blockchain-payments-enter-trials-Friday?n_cid=NARAN012Nissen, H, Damerow, P and Englund, R K (1993) *Archaic Bookkeeping: Early writing techniques of economic administration in the ancient Near East,* University of Chicago Press, London

Peters, G and Panayi, E (2015) [accessed 15 February 2018] Understanding Modern Banking Ledgers through Blockchain Technologies: Future of Transaction Processing and Smart Contracts on the Internet of Money, *Cornell University*, 18/11 [Online] https://arxiv.org/pdf/1511.05740.pdf

Russo, C (2017) [accessed 15 February 2018] Disrupting Finance: How the EU Payment Services Directive (PSD2) Will Impact the European Banking System, *Roland Berger*, 08/02 [Online] https://www.rolandberger.com/en/press/Disrupting-Finance-How-the-EU-Payment-Services-Directive-(PSD2)-will-impact-the-2.html

Skinner, C (2016) *Value Web: How FinTech firms are using mobile and blockchain technologies to create the internet of value*, Marshall Cavendish Business, Singapore

Son, H, Levitt, H and Louis, B (2017) [accessed 15 February 2018] Jamie Dimon Slams Bitcoin as a 'Fraud', *Bloomberg Technology*, 12/09 [Online] https://www.bloomberg.com/news/articles/2017-09-12/jpmorgan-s-ceo-says-he-d-fire-traders-who-bet-on-fraud-bitcoin

Swan, M (2015) *Blockchain: Blueprint for a new economy*, O'Reilly Media Inc, Sebastopol, CA

Tapscott, D and Tapscott, A (2016) *Blockchain Revolution: How the technology behind bitcoin is changing money, business, and the world,* Penguin Random House, New York

Umeh, J (2016) Blockchain: double bubble or double trouble, *ITNOW*, March, pp 58–61

Van De Mieroop, M (1992) *Society and Enterprise in Old Babylonian Ur*, Reimer-Verlag, Berlin

Wild, J, Arnold, M and Stafford, P (2015) [accessed 15 February 2018] Technology: Banks Seek the Key to Blockchain: Financial Groups Race to Harness the Power of the Bitcoin Infrastructure to Slash Costs, *Financial Times*, 1/11 [Online] https://next.ft.com/content/eb1f8256-7b4b-11e5-a1fe-567b37f80b64

Chapter 3

Accenture (2013) [accessed 15 February 2018] Banking 2020: As the Storm Abates, North American Banks Must Chart a New Course to Capture Emerging Opportunities, *Report* [Online] https://www.accenture.com/gr-en/~/media/Accenture/Conversion-Assets/DotCom/Documents/Global/PDF/Industries_3/Accenture-Banking-2020-POV.pdf

Bikker, J and Haaf, K (2002) Competition, concentration and their relationship: an empirical analysis of the banking industry, *Journal of Banking & Finance*, **26**, pp 2191–214

Brynjolfsson, E and McAfee, A (2014) *The Second Machine Age: Work, progress and prosperity in a time of brilliant technologies*, W W Norton & Company, New York

Chesbrough, H (2003) The governance and performance of Xerox's technology spin-off companies, *Research Policy*, **32** (3), pp 403–21

Christensen, C and Bower, J (1996) Customer power, strategic investment, and the failure of leading firms, *Strategic Management Journal*, **17** (3), pp 197–218

Citi GPS (2016) [accessed 15 February 2018] Digital Disruption: How Fintech is Forcing Banking to a Tipping Point [Online] https://www.nist.gov/sites/default/files/documents/2016/09/15/citi_rfi_response.pdf

Danneels, E (2004) Disruptive Technology Reconsidered: A Critique and Research Agenda, *Journal of Product Innovation Management*, **21**, pp 246–58

David, P (1989) Computer and dynamo: the modern productivity paradox in a not-too-distant mirror, University of Stanford, Palo Alto, CA: Working Paper Center for Economic Policy Research

Deloitte (2016) Blockchain and contactless card payments, *Nilson Report*, November, **1099**, pp 6–7

Deloitte and Efma (2016) [accessed 10 October 2018] Out of the Blocks: Blockchain: From Hype to Prototype [Online] https://www.efma.com/study/detail/25582

Deutsche Bank (2016) [accessed 15 February 2018] White Paper: FinTech 2.0: Creating New Opportunities through Strategic Alliance [Online] http://cib.db.com/docs_new/GTB_FinTech_Whitepaper_A4_SCREEN.pdf

Estrin, J (2015) [accessed 15 February 2018] Kodak's First Digital Moment, *New York Times*, 12/8 [Online] https://lens.blogs.nytimes.com/2015/08/12/kodaks-first-digital-moment/?_r=0#

Euro Banking Association (2015) [accessed 15 February 2018] Cryptotechnologies, a Major IT Innovation and Catalyst for Change: 4 Categories, 4 Applications and 4 Scenarios: An Exploration for Transaction Banking and Payment Professionals, *Report*, 11/05 [Online] http://www.the-blockchain.com/docs/Euro%20Banking%20Association%20-%20Cryptotechnologies%20-%20%20a%20major%20IT%20innovation.pdf

Finextra and IBM (2016) [accessed 15 February 2018] Banking on Blockchain: Charting the Progress of Distributed Ledger Technology in Financial Services, *White Paper*, January [Online] https://www.finextra.com/finextra-downloads/surveys/documents/32e19ab4-2d9c-4862-8416-d3be94161c6d/banking%20on%20blockchain.pdf

Frost and Sullivan (2016) [accessed 15 February 2018] Global Rating of Direct Banks 2016: Benchmarking Direct Banks' Client Base, *Report*, October [Online] https://static.tinkoff.ru/news/2016/2016-10-04-global-rating-of-direct-banks.pdf

Glaser, P (1988) Using Technology for Competitive Advantage: The ATM Experience at Citicorp, in *Managing Innovation: Cases from the services industries*, ed B Guile and J Quinn, National Academy, Washington DC

Government Accountability Office (2013) [accessed 15 February 2018] Financial Institutions: Causes and Consequences of Recent Community Bank Failures: Testimony Before the Committee on Banking, Housing, and Urban Affairs, US Senate, *Statement of Lawrance L Evans*, 13/06 [Online] http://www.gao.gov/assets/660/655193.pdf

Grove, A (1996) [accessed 15 February 2018] *Only the Paranoid Survive*, Doubleday, New York

HBS (nd) [accessed 10 October 2018] [Online] https://www.hbs.edu/faculty/Pages/profile.aspx?facId=6532

Heires, K (2016) The risks and rewards of blockchain technology, *Risk Management*, (March), pp 4–7

Hileman, G (2016) [accessed 15 February 2018] State of bitcoin and blockchain 2016, *CoinDesk*, 01/02 [Online] http://www.CoinDesk.com/state-of-bitcoin-blockchain-2016/

Hill, C (1997) Establishing a standard: competitive strategy and technology standards in winner takes all industries, *Academy of Management Executive,* **11**, pp 7–25

Iansiti, M, McFarlan, W and Westerman, G (2003) Leveraging the Incumbent's Advantage, *MIT Sloan Management Review*, **44** (4), pp 58–64

Irrera, A (2017) [accessed 15 February 2018] Blockchain Consortium Hyperledger Loses Members, Funding: Documents, *Reuters*, 15/12 [Online] https://www.reuters.com/article/us-blockchain-consortium/blockchain-consortium-hyperledger-loses-members-funding-documents-idUSKBN1E92O4

King, B (2014) *Breaking Banks: The Innovators, Rogues, and Strategists Rebooting Banking*, John Wiley & Sons, Singapore

Levitt, T (1965) [accessed 15 February 2018] Exploit the Product Life Cycle, *Harvard Business Review*, **43** (6), pp 81–94 [Online] https://hbr.org/1965/11/exploit-the-product-life-cycle

Mac, R (2014) [accessed 10 April 2016] PayPal Takes Baby Step Toward Bitcoin, Partners with Cryptocurrency Processors, *Forbes* [Online] https://www.forbes.com/sites/ryanmac/2014/09/23/paypal-takes-small-step-toward-bitcoin-partners-with-cryptocurrency-processors/#410b7381311b

Miller, D (1990) *The Icarus Paradox*, Harper Business, New York

Mills, QM (1996) [accessed 15 February 2018] The Decline and Rise of IBM, *Sloan Review*, 15/07 [Online] https://sloanreview.mit.edu/article/the-decline-and-rise-of-ibm/

Porter, M (1979) How competitive forces shape industry, *Michael E. Porter on Competition and Strategy – Collection of Articles* (1991), Harvard Business Press, Cambridge, MA, pp 3–11

Porter, M (1980, reprint 1998) *Competitive Strategy: Techniques for analyzing industries and competitors*, Free Press, New York

Porter, M (1985) *Competitive Advantage*, Free Press, New York

Quinn, J and Baily, M (1994) Information technology: increasing productivity in services, *The Academy of Management Executive*, **8** (3), 28–48

Redman, J (2016) [accessed 15 February 2018] MasterCard Gets Serious with Four Blockchain Patents, *bitcoin.com*, 2/12 [Online] https://news.bitcoin.com/mastercard-four-blockchain-patents/

Shapiro, C (1989) The Theory of Business Strategy, *RAND Journal of Economics*, **20** (1), pp 125–37

Skinner, C (2016) *Value Web: How FinTech firms are using mobile and blockchain technologies to create the internet of value*, Marshall Cavendish Business, Singapore

Statista (2017) [accessed 20 August 2018] Number of Current Account Customers Gained and Lost By Leading Banks in the United Kingdom (UK) Via 'Current Account Switch Service' (CASS) in the Second Quarter 2017 [Online] https://www.statista.com/statistics/417599/current-account-switching-by-bank-gain-or-loss-uk/

Statista (2018) [accessed 15 February 2018] PayPal's Annual Revenue From 2010 to 2017 [Online] https://www.statista.com/statistics/382619/paypal-annual-revenue/

Sull, D (2003) *Revival of the Fittest: Why good companies go bad and how great managers remake them*, Harvard Business School Press, Boston, MA

Sutton, J (1992) Implementing game theoretical models in industrial economies, *Recent Developments in the Theory of Industrial Organization*, ed Alfredo Del Monte, pp 19–33, University of Michigan Press, Ann Arbor, MI

Synergy Research Group (2016) [accessed 15 February 2018] Amazon Leads; Microsoft, IBM & Google Chase; Others Trail, *Report*, 01/08 [Online] https://www.srgresearch.com/articles/amazon-leads-microsoft-ibm-google-chase-others-trail

Teece, D, Pisano, G and Shuen, A (1997) Dynamic capabilities and strategic management, *Strategic Management Journal*, **18**, pp 509–33

The Economist (2012) [accessed 15 February 2018] Remittances: Over the Sea and Far Away, *The Economist*, 19/05 [Online] www.economist.com/node/21554740

USBankLocations.com (2018) [accessed 15 February 2018] Banks Ranked by Number of Branches [Online] http://www.usbanklocations.com/bank-rank/number-of-branches.html

Utterback, J (1994) *Mastering the Dynamics of Innovation*, Harvard Business School Press, Boston, MA

Wolf, J (1912) *Die Volkswirtschaft der Gegenwart und Zukunft*, A Deichert, Leipzig

Chapter 4

ACI Worldwide and Aite Group (2017) [accessed 15 February 2018] Global Consumer Survey: Consumer Trust and Security Perceptions [Online] https://www.aciworldwide.com/-/media/files/collateral/trends/2017-global-consumer-survey-consumer-trust-and-security-perceptions.pdf

Brand Finance (2017) [accessed 15 February 2018] Global 500 2017: The Annual Report on the World's Most Valuable Brands [Online] http://brandfinance.com/images/upload/global_500_2017_locked_website.pdf

Capgemini, LinkedIn and Efma (2018) [accessed 15 February 2018] World Fintech Report 2018, 27/02 [Online] https://www.capgemini.com/wp-content/uploads/2018/02/world-fintech-report-wftr-2018.pdf

Chandy, R and Tellis, G (2000) The incumbent's curse? Incumbency, size, and radical product innovation, *Journal of Marketing*, **64** (3), pp 1–17

China Economic Net (2017) [accessed 15 April 2018] China Outpaces US on Mobile Payments, 15/02 [Online] http://en.ce.cn/main/latest/201702/15/t20170215_20244626.shtml?utm_source=eNewsletterPro&utm_medium=email&utm_campaign=Smarter_Facility_Management_with_Smart_ID_Badging__1544

Christensen, C and Bower, J (1996) Customer power, strategic investment, and the failure of leading firms, *Strategic Management Journal*, **17** (3), pp 197–218

CGI Group (2017) [accessed 15 April 2018] CGI Global Payments Research 2017: Key Highlights and Observations [Online] https://www.cgi.com/sites/default/files/pdf/cgi-global-payments-research.pdf

Citi GPS (2016) [accessed 15 February 2018] Digital Disruption: How Fintech is Forcing Banking to a Tipping Point, March [Online] https://www.nist.gov/sites/default/files/documents/2016/09/15/citi_rfi_response.pdf

Coinometrics (2015) in Skinner, C (2016) *Value Web: How FinTech firms are using mobile and blockchain technologies to create the internet of value*, Marshall Cavendish Business, Singapore

Dahinden, U (2006) *Framing: Eine integrative theorie der massenkommunikation*, UVK, Konstanz

De, Nikhilesh (2017) [accessed 15 May 2018] Apple Patent Filing Hints at Blockchain Use, *Coindesk*, 07/12 [Online] https://www.coindesk.com/apple-patent-filing-hints-blockchain-timestamp-use/

Deutsche Bank (2016) [accessed 15 February 2018] White Paper: FinTech 2.0: Creating New Opportunities through Strategic Alliance, February [Online] http://cib.db.com/insights-and-initiatives/white-papers/FinTech_2_0_Creating_new_opportunities_through_strategic_alliance.htm

Dimon, J (2014) [accessed 15 February 2018] JP Morgan Chase & Co, Annual Report 2013, 09/04 [Online] http://online.wsj.com/public/resources/documents/040913dimon.pdf

Goldman Sachs (2015) The future of finance: the rise of the new shadow bank, *Equity Research*, 3 March

Heggestuen, J (2014) [accessed 15 February 2018] Alipay Overtakes PayPal as the Largest Mobile Payments Platform in the World, *Business Insider*, 11/02 [Online] http://www.businessinsider.de/

alipay-overtakes-paypal-as-the-largest-mobile-payments-platform-in-the-world-2014-2?r=US&IR=T

Heires, K (2016) The risks and rewards of blockchain technology, *Risk Management*, 1 March, pp 4–7

Klepper, S and Simons, K (2000) Dominance by birthright: entry to prior radio producers and competitive ramifications in the US television receiver industry, *Strategic Management Journal*, **21** (10–11), pp 997–1016

KPMG (2017) [accessed 15 February 2018] The Pulse of Fintech Q4 2016: Global Analysis of Investment in Fintech, 21/02 [Online] https://assets.kpmg.com/content/dam/kpmg/xx/pdf/2017/02/pulse-of-fintech-q4-2016.pdf

McKinsey Financial Services Practice (2017) [accessed 15 February 2018] Payments: On the Crest of the Fintech Wave, May [Online] https://www.mckinsey.com/industries/financial-services/our-insights/payments-on-the-crest-of-the-fintech-wave

Methe, D *et al* (1997) The underemphasized role of diversifying entrants and industry incumbents as the sources of major innovations, in *Strategic Discovery: Competing in new arenas*, ed H Thomas, D O'Neal and R Alvarado, pp 99–116, Wiley, New York

Nykiel, T (2014) [accessed 8 May 2018] Here's Why The Biggest Banks Are Pushing Apple Pay, *Business Insider*, 25/09 [Online] http://www.businessinsider.com/the-biggest-banks-are-pushing-apple-pay-2014-9?IR=T

Porter, M (1979) How Competitive Forces Shape Industry, in *Michael E. Porter on Competition and Strategy – Collection of Articles*, Harvard Business Press, Cambridge, MA, pp 3–11

PYMNTS (2017) [accessed 8 May 2018] Digital Wallets Dominated Social Media Conversations In 2016, 01/03 [Online] http://www.pymnts.com/news/security-and-risk/2017/digital-wallets-dominated-social-media-conversations-in-2016/

PYMNTS/INFOSCOUT (2018a) [accessed 8 May 2018] Mobile Wallet Adoption: Where Are We Now? [Online] https://www.pymnts.com/mobile-wallet-adoption-statistics/

PYMNTS.COM/INFOSCOUT (2018b) [accessed 8 May 2018] Apple Pay Wallet Adoption: Where Are We Now? [Online] https://www.pymnts.com/apple-pay-adoption/

Rothaermel, F (2001) Incumbents' advantage through exploiting complementary assets via interfirm cooperation, *Strategic Management Journal*, **22** (6–7), pp 687–99

Skinner, C (2016) *Value Web: How FinTech firms are using mobile and blockchain technologies to create the internet of value*, Marshall Cavendish Business, Singapore

Statista (2017) [accessed 15 May 2018] Number of Apps Available in Leading App Stores as of March 2017 [Online] https://www.statista.com/statistics/276623/number-of-apps-available-in-leading-app-stores/

Statista (2018) [accessed 15 May 2018] Funding and Investment of Blockchain Startup Companies Worldwide from 2012 to 2017 (In Million US Dollars) [Online] https://www.statista.com/statistics/621207/worldwide-blockchain-startup-financing-history/

Sundararajan, S (2018) [accessed 8 May 2018] Search Giant Baidu Launches Blockchain-as-a-Service Platform, 12/01 [Online] https://www.coindesk.com/search-giant-baidu-launches-blockchain-as-a-service-platform/

Synergy Research Group (2016) [accessed 15 February 2018] Amazon Leads; Microsoft, IBM & Google Chase; Others Trail, *Report*, 01/08 [Online] https://www.srgresearch.com/articles/amazon-leads-microsoft-ibm-google-chase-others-trail

The Economist (2017) [accessed 20 May 2018] Schumpeter: Harvard Business School Risks Going From Great To Good: A Confidential Memorandum of Warning To Its Senior Faculty, *The Economist*, 04/05 [Online] http://www.economist.com/news/business/21721681-confidential-memorandum-warning-its-senior-faculty-harvard-business-school-risks-going

Walmart (2015) [accessed 11 May 2018] Walmart Introduces Walmart Pay: Pay With Any iOS or Android Smartphone, Any Major Payment Type and at Any Checkout Lane – All Through the Walmart App, press release, 10/12 [Online] http://news.walmart.com/news-archive/2015/12/10/walmart-introduces-walmart-pay

Webster, K (2017) [accessed 20 April 2017] An Inconvenient Apple Pay Truth, *PYMNTS*, 10/04 [Online] http://www.pymnts.com/news/payment-methods/2017/apple-pay-adoption-down-and-so-is-the-hype-mobile-pay-usage/

Wild, J, Arnold, M and Stafford, P (2015) [accessed 15 February 2018] Technology: Banks Seek the Key to Blockchain: Financial Groups Race to Harness the Power of the Bitcoin Infrastructure to Slash Costs, *Financial Times*, 1/11 [Online] https://next.ft.com/content/eb1f8256-7b4b-11e5-a1fe-567b37f80b64

Yuanyuan, D (2016) [accessed 10 May 2018] Alibaba, Baidu and Tencent and Their New Online Banks, 26/12 [Online] http://fintechranking.com/2016/12/26/alibaba-baidu-and-tencent-and-their-new-online-banks/

Chapter 5

Burke, A, van Steel, A and Thurik, R (2009) Blue ocean *versus* competitive strategy: theory and evidence, *ERIM Report Series Research in Management*, pp 1–25

Capgemini, LinkedIn and Efma (2018) [accessed 15 May 2018] World Fintech Report 2018, 27/02 [Online] https://www.capgemini.com/wp-content/uploads/2018/02/world-fintech-report-wftr-2018.pdf

Citi GPS (2016) [accessed 15 February 2018] Digital Disruption: How Fintech is Forcing Banking to a Tipping Point, March [Online] https://www.nist.gov/sites/default/files/documents/2016/09/15/citi_rfi_response.pdf

Danneels, E (2004) Disruptive technology reconsidered: a critique and research agenda, *Journal of Product Innovation Management*, **21**, pp 246–58

Deutsche Bank (2016) [accessed 15 February 2018] White Paper: FinTech 2.0: Creating New Opportunities Through Strategic Alliance, February [Online] http://cib.db.com/insights-and-initiatives/white-papers/FinTech_2_0_Creating_new_opportunities_through_strategic_alliance.htm

Goddard, J (1997) The architecture of core competence, *Business Strategy Review*, **8** (1), pp 43–52

Hansen, G and Wernerfelt, B (1989) Determinants of firm performance: the relative performance of economic and organizational factors, *Strategic Management Journal*, **10** (5), pp 399–411

Kahn, J (2016) [accessed 15 February 2018] London's Lonely Unicorn: Two Frugal Expats and Their Billion Dollar Startup, *Bloomberg*, 13/06 [Online] https://www.bloomberg.com/news/articles/2016-06-13/london-s-lonely-unicorn-two-frugal-expats-and-their-billion-dollar-startup

Khiaonarong, T and Liebenau, J (2009) *Banking on Innovation: Modernization of payment systems*, Physica-Verlag (Springer), Heidelberg

Kim, C and Mauborgne, R (2005) *Blue Ocean Strategy: How to create uncontested market space and make competition irrelevant*, Harvard Business Review Press, Boston, MA

King, B (2014) *Breaking Banks: The innovators, rogues, and strategists rebooting banking*, John Wiley & Sons, Singapore

Lewis, A and McKone, D (2016) *Edge Strategy: A new mindset for profitable growth*, Harvard Business Review Press, Boston, MA

Mata, F, Fuerst W and Barney, J (1995) Information technology and sustained competitive advantage: a resource-based analysis, *MIS Quarterly*, **19** (December), pp 487–505

Nguyen, HL (2014) [accessed 15 May 2018] Do bank branches still matter? The effect of closings on local economic outcomes, *Massachusetts Institute of Technology Working Paper*, December [Online] https://www.rhsmith.umd.edu/files/Documents/Departments/Finance/seminarspring2015/nguyen.pdf

Peachey, K (2017) [accessed 15 May 2018] Mobiles 'fast replacing' bank branch visits, BBC, 28/06 [Online] http://www.bbc.com/news/business-40421868

Penrose, E (1959) *The Theory of the Growth of the Firm*, Basil Blackwell, London

Porter, M (1979) How competitive forces shape industry, in *Michael E. Porter on Competition and Strategy – Collection of Articles* (1991), pp 3–11, Harvard Business Press, Cambridge, MA

Porter, M (1998 [1980]) *Competitive Strategy: Techniques for analyzing industries and competitors*, Free Press, New York

Porter, M (1985) *Competitive Advantage*, Free Press, New York

Powell, T (1992a) Organizational alignment as competitive advantage, *Strategic Management Journal*, **13** (2), pp 119–34

Powell, T (1992b) Strategic planning as competitive advantage, *Strategic Management Journal*, **13** (7), pp 551–58

Prahalad, C and Hamel, G (1990) The core competence of the corporation, *Harvard Business Review*, **68**, pp 79–90

Rangan, K and Lee, K (2010) [accessed 15 February 2018] HBS Case: Mobile Banking for the Unbanked, *Harvard Business Review*, 17/09 [Online] https://hbr.org/product/mobile-banking-for-the-unbanked/an/511049-PDF-ENG

Rumelt, R (1991) How much does industry matter?, *Strategic Management Journal*, **12** (3), pp 556–70

Schumpeter, J (1942) *Capitalism, Socialism, and Democracy*, Harper & Brothers, New York

Teece, D, Pisano, G and Shuen, A (1997) Dynamic capabilities and strategic management, *Strategic Management Journal*, **18**, pp 509–33

Trefis Team (2017) [accessed 15 May 2018] The Five Largest US Banks Hold More Than 40% Of All Deposits, *Forbes*, 14/12 [Online] https://www.forbes.com/sites/greatspeculations/2017/12/14/the-five-largest-u-s-banks-hold-more-than-40-of-all-deposits/#709058f116aa

Tripsas, M (1997) Unraveling the process of creative destruction: complimentary assets and incumbent survival in the typesetter industry, *Strategic Management Journal*, **18** (summer), pp 119–42

Vikas, M, Sarkees, M and Murshed, F (2008) [accessed 15 February 2018] The Right Way to Manage Unprofitable Customers, *Harvard Business Review*, **86** (4), pp 94–102 [Online] https://hbr.org/2008/04/the-right-way-to-manage-unprofitable-customers

World Bank Group (2015) [accessed 15 February 2018] The Global Findex Database 2014: measuring financial inclusion around the world, *Policy Research Working Paper 7255* [Online] http://www-wds.worldbank.org/external/default/WDSContentServer/WDSP/IB/2015/10/19/090224b08315413c/2_0/Rendered/PDF/The0Global0Fin0ion0around0the0world.pdf#page=3

World Bank (2018) [accessed 15 May 2018] Commercial Bank Branches (Per 100,000 Adults) [Online] https://data.worldbank.org/indicator/FB.CBK.BRCH.P5?locations=US

Chapter 6

ACI Worldwide and Aite Group (2017) [accessed 15 May 2018] Global Consumer Survey: Consumer Trust and Security Perceptions, February [Online] https://www.aciworldwide.com/-/media/files/collateral/trends/2017-global-consumer-survey-consumer-trust-and-security-perceptions.pdf

Baden-Fuller, C and Haefliger, S (2013) Business models and technological innovation, *Long Range Planning*, **46**, pp 419–26

BBC (2004) [accessed 15 May 2018] Passwords Revealed By Sweet Deal, 20/04 [Online] http://news.bbc.co.uk/2/hi/technology/3639679.stm

Capgemini, LinkedIn and Efma (2018) [accessed 15 May 2018] World Fintech Report 2018, 27/02 [Online] https://www.capgemini.com/wp-content/uploads/2018/02/world-fintech-report-wftr-2018.pdf

Danneels, E (2004) Disruptive technology reconsidered: a critique and research agenda, *Journal of Product Innovation Management*, **21**, pp 246–58

Forrester (2016) in Skinner, C (2016) *Value Web: How FinTech firms are using mobile and blockchain technologies to create the internet of value*, Marshall Cavendish Business, Singapore

Grove, A (1996) *Only the Paranoid Survive*, Doubleday, New York

Libert, B, Beck, M and Wind, J (2016a) [accessed 15 May 2018] Network Revolution: Creating Value Through Platforms, People, and Technology, 14/04 [Online] http://knowledge.wharton.upenn.edu/article/the-network-revolution-creating-value-through-platforms-people-and-digital-technology/

Libert, B, Beck M and Wind, J (2016b) [accessed 15 May 2018] How Blockchain Technology Will Disrupt Financial Services Firms, 24/05 [Online] http://knowledge.wharton.upenn.edu/article/blockchain-technology-will-disrupt-financial-services-firms/

Porter, M (1979) How competitive forces shape industry, in *Michael E Porter on Competition and Strategy – Collection of Articles*, Harvard Business Press, Cambridge, MA, pp 3–11

PrivatBank (2016) [accessed 15 May 2018] PrivatBank is One of the First Banks Worldwide to Offer API-Based and Open Source IT-Architecture Services, *Value Web*, 04/05 [Online] https://en.privatbank.ua/news/-privatbank-is-one-of-the-first-banks-worldwide-to-offer-api-based-and-open-source-it-architecture-services-chris-skinner-value-web/

Rochet, J and Tirole, J (2006) Two-sided markets: a progress report, *Rand Journal of Economics*, **37** (3), pp 645–67

Skinner, C (2016) *Value Web: How FinTech firms are using mobile and blockchain technologies to create the internet of value*, Marshall Cavendish Business, Singapore

Stocco, G (2015) [accessed 15 May 2018] The Finanser Interviews: Guga Stocco, Head of Strategy and Innovation, Banco Original, August, Brazil [Online] https://thefinanser.com/2015/08/the-finanser-interviews-guga-stocco-head-of-strategy-and-innovation-banco-original-brazil.html/

Traynor *et al* (2013) [accessed 15 May 2018] Cyprus Bailout Deal With EU Closes Bank and Seizes Large Deposits, *The Guardian*, 25 March

[Online] https://www.theguardian.com/world/2013/mar/25/cyprus-bailout-deal-eu-closes-bank

Tversky, A and Kahneman, D (1981) The framing of decision and the psychology of choice, *Science*, **211** (4481), pp 453–58

Wiens, R (2018) Erste Group will neue Märkte erobern, *Salzburger Nachrichten*, 1 March

Chapter 7

Browne, R (2017) [accessed 15 May 2018] Big Transaction Fees Are a Problem For Bitcoin — But There Could Be a Solution, CNBC, 19/12 [Online] https://www.cnbc.com/2017/12/19/big-transactions-fees-are-a-problem-for-bitcoin.html

Christin, N (2013) Traveling the silk road: a measurement analysis of a large anonymous marketplace, *Proceedings of the 22nd International World Wide Web Conference, Rio de Janeiro*, pp 213–24

FDIC – Federal Deposit Insurance Corporation (2016) [accessed 15 May 2018] 2015 FDIC National Survey of Unbanked and Underbanked Households, 20/10 [Online] https://www.fdic.gov/householdsurvey/2015/2015report.pdf

Ferguson, N (2008) *The Ascent of Money: A Financial History of the World*, Penguin Books, London

Foundation Capital (2014) [accessed 15 May 2018] A Trillion Dollar Market By the People, For the People: How Marketplace Lending Will Remake Banking As We Know [Online] https://foundationcapital.com/wp-content/uploads/2016/08/TDMFinTech_whitepaper.pdf

FRED – Federal Reserve Bank of St Louis (2017a) [accessed 15 May 2018] Remittance Inflows to GDP for Haiti (DDOI11HTA156NWDB), 30/08 [Online] https://fred.stlouisfed.org/series/DDOI11HTA156NWDB

FRED – Federal Reserve Bank of St Louis (2017b) [accessed 15 May 2018] Remittance Inflows to GDP for Philippines (DDOI11PHA156NWDB), 30/08 [Online] https://fred.stlouisfed.org/series/DDOI11HTA156NWDB

Glaser, P (1988) Using Technology for Competitive Advantage: The ATM Experience at Citicorp, in *Managing Innovation: Cases from the services industries*, ed B Guile and J Quinn, National Academy, Washington DC

Hileman, G (2015) [accessed 15 May 2018] The Bitcoin Market Potential Index, *Financial Cryptography and Data Security*, pp 92–93 [Online] https://link.springer.com/chapter/10.1007%2F978-3-662-48051-9_7

MacAskill, A, Jessop, S and Cohn, C (2017) [accessed 15 May 2018] Exclusive – Reuters Survey: 10,000 UK Finance Jobs Affected in Brexit's First Wave, *Reuters*, 18/09 [Online] https://uk.reuters.com/article/uk-britain-eu-jobs-exclusive/exclusive-reuters-survey-10000-uk-finance-jobs-affected-in-brexits-first-wave-idUKKCN1BT1EQ

Rangan, K and Lee, K (2010) [accessed 15 May 2018] HBS Case: Mobile Banking for the Unbanked, *Harvard Business Review*, 17/09 [Online] https://hbr.org/product/mobile-banking-for-the-unbanked/an/511049-PDF-ENG

Santander, Oliver Wyman and Anthemis Group (2015) [accessed 15 February 2018] The Fintech 2.0 Paper: Rebooting Financial Services [Online] http://santanderinnoventures.com/wp-content/uploads/2015/06/The-Fintech-2-0-Paper.pdf

SelectUSA (2016) [accessed 15 May 2018] Financial Services Spotlight: The Financial Services Industry in the United States [Online] https://www.selectusa.gov/financial-services-industry-united-states

Suri T and Jack, W (2016) [accessed 15 May 2018] The Long-Run Poverty and Gender Impacts of Mobile Money, *Science*, **354** (6317), pp 1288–92 [Online] http://science.sciencemag.org/content/354/6317/1288.full

The Economist (2017) [accessed 20 May 2018] Changing Maps: How the Shape of Global Banking Has Turned Upside Down, *The Economist*, 28/08 [Online] https://www.economist.com/news/finance-and-economics/21727088-american-and-european-banks-stay-more-home-chinese-ones-extend-their-reach-how

Umeh, J (2016) Blockchain: Double Bubble or Double Trouble?, *ITNOW*, pp 58–61 (March)

World Bank Group (2015) [accessed 15 February 2018] The Global Findex Database 2014: Measuring Financial Inclusion Around the World, *Policy Research Working Paper 7255* [Online] http://www-wds.worldbank.org/external/default/WDSContentServer/WDSP/IB/2015/10/19/090224b08315413c/2_0/Rendered/PDF/The0Global0Fin0ion0around0the0world.pdf#page=3

Index

NB: page numbers in *italic* indicate figures or tables